ST. JOSEPH'S DAY

IN NEW ORLEANS

ST. JOSEPH'S DAY

IN NEW ORLEANS

Laura Guccione

Louisiana State University Press
Baton Rouge

Published with the assistance of the V. Ray Cardozier Fund

Published by Louisiana State University Press
lsupress.org

Manufactured in the United States of America
First printing

DESIGNER: Michelle A. Neustrom
TYPEFACE: Garamond Premier Pro
PRINTER AND BINDER: Sheridan Books, Inc.

The manufacturer's authorized representative in the EU for product safety is Mare Nostrum Group B.V., Doelen 72, 4831 GR Breda, The Netherlands.
Email: gpsr@mare-nostrum.co.uk.

JACKET ILLUSTRATION: *St. Joseph's Day Masked Ball*, by Andrew LaMar Hopkins.

Cataloging-in-Publication Data are available from the Library of Congress.

ISBN 978-0-8071-8641-1 (cloth: alk. paper) — ISBN 978-0-8071-8828-6 (pdf) —
ISBN 978-0-8071-8827-9 (epub)

To Ann

Contents

Illustrations

Acknowledgments

Honestly, I never imagined I would write a book, especially an academic one! What an exciting but lonely journey it has been.

I am incredibly grateful for the amazing support I received along the way. First, I would like to give a heartfelt thank you to my wonderful mother, Joan Guccione, and my fantastic sisters, Ann Guccione and Jean Guccione, whose love and encouragement kept me going, especially during my time of unemployment. I would also like to thank Dean Kageler, Ann's boyfriend, who created an escape from the city, and Jean's husband, Bobby Levins, who listened as I explained what I had found in my research. And to my brothers Steven Guccione and Michael Guccione, who told me that writing this book was worth the time and effort. To Gretchen Grisbaum, the sister that I got stuck with, as she would say to me. She passed away before I finished, but she helped me complete what I started. I am deeply thankful to my friends who not only helped with editing but also lifted my spirits and kept my sanity intact—Connie Atkinson, Elisa Speranza, Kathryn O'Dwyer, Dana Logsdon, Meg Garvey, Darcy McKinnon and her mom, Rhea, Carin Baas and Brett Deneau, Chelsea Nelson, Colleen Stephens, Christy Beshears, Heather Cusimano, Heather Veneziano, Bethany Bultman, Ellis Anderson, Laura Ferrara, Loretta Jackson, Deborah Toscano, Tatiana Jurzak, Dama Fountain and Royce Osborn, Marisa Vargo, Nikira Johnson, Nikki McCoy, Jari Honora, Joe Darensbourg, Shawanda Williams, Albert Devall Dumas, Angi Cinquemano, Rick Delaup, Greg Osborn, Renea Pellegrino, Al and Vickie Kennedy, Dianne Honoré, Darryl Montana, Poppy Tooker, Christine Fontana, Carol Millan, and Bloody Mary, Voodoo scholar. I feel lucky to have such an incredible circle of support. And to Jessica Dorman, whose words about the book's potential helped more than she could imagine. To my French Quarter Fest family: Greg Schatz, for hiring me when I really needed a job, and to my crew—Willie Kidd, Sophie Miller, Kevin Reed, and my Cajun-Zydeco musician friends—who gave me some much-needed social time and encouraged me year after year to keep with it.

A special thanks to Andrew LaMar Hopkins for creating the cover art. It is even more magnificent than I could have imagined. You are proof that hard work can lead to good things. And to Denise Augustine, who made me get up and out of the house for our daily walk and talk. Thanks to Allen and Becky Freedman, not only for the friendly lunches but also for the financial advice when I needed it most. To my long-lost cousins Gerald Emelle and Natalie Murry. And Nancy, Sarah, and Dylan at the Alvar Branch of the New Orleans Public Library—I think I saw you more than anyone except my family, my USPS guy, Earnest Wells, and Jason Hardesty from UPS. And to Amanda Fallis, who found what I needed at the eleventh hour. Without the public libraries in New Orleans and Baton Rouge, the Historic New Orleans Collection, the libraries of UNO, Tulane, and Loyola, and especially the Cammie G. Henry Research Center at Northwestern State University of Louisiana, none of this would have been possible. Free resources enable great discoveries for everyone.

And to Jenny Keegan from LSU Press for giving me a chance.

ST. JOSEPH'S DAY
IN NEW ORLEANS

INTRODUCTION

It would be difficult to find any place in the world
where St. Joseph's Day is celebrated more
than it is in New Orleans.

—A. L. DUNN

On Sunday, August 28, 2005, my sister and I jammed into her Saturn with our mom, two friends, and our cat Bootsy. Hurricane Katrina was heading our way, and this was the first time we had ever evacuated New Orleans for a storm. I did not want to go, but, as my sister pointed out correctly, we had to think of our mom. Even if the storm damage was minor, we would not have electricity, and it was in the depths of summer in New Orleans, and the weather was not nice. That year had been good for me. I owned a shop with my sister in the French Quarter that specialized in handmade masks, including our own creations. Our business was gaining recognition after being featured on local and national television shows, and I was bartending one night a week on Frenchmen Street for the fun of it. A week or so before Katrina, I had told the other bartender, JW Rogers, a lanky, handsome guy from Texas, that this was a magical time. Frenchmen Street was beginning to be discovered by tourists, but that night, most of the patrons were locals. The New Orleans Jazz Vipers played on that warm, humid Friday night. As I surveyed the bar, I saw faces I knew well, including some notable musicians who had stopped by to sit in for a song or two or to have a nightcap after their shows elsewhere, and there were also a few tourists in the know. This scene would change drastically in just a few weeks.

Earlier that year, my interest in creating a St. Joseph's Day altar, a tradition tied to my Sicilian roots but one that was fading in popularity at the time, had led me through a mutual friend, Leslie Lowe, to Father Jerome LeDoux, the celebrated parish priest at St. Augustine Church in the Tremé. I was nervous as I was on my way to meet him, for reasons I did not understand then. Even though I was raised Catholic, I was no longer practicing—often joking, like so many people, about being a recovering Catholic—so perhaps that Catholic guilt was creeping up. Would he ask me where I went to church? How would I answer him? Instead, he greeted me with a big smile and a hug, immediately quashing all my fears and guilt. We hit it off right away, both being straightforward and full of energy. He would go on to become an essential part of my life in multiple ways.

I asked Father LeDoux to allow my sister Ann, my friend Jackie, and me to build a St. Joseph's Day altar in the church for the saint's feast day, March 19. He was intrigued; he thought about it briefly and gave us his blessing. We told him that we would do all the work, but his parishioners were welcome to join in. He flashed his bright smile and said, "What do we have to lose?" A large marble statue of St. Joseph, positioned on the right side of the church, was waiting for an altar.

We started organizing.

We thought the inaugural altar would be a small neighborhood affair, but we were pleasantly surprised that as word got out, people from the Tremé and friends at restaurants in the French Quarter wanted to help. We served food from many places, including famous restaurants like K-Paul's and Nola (Emeril Lagasse's flagship restaurant in New Orleans), but what touched my heart were the gifts of food from so many older, long-term Black residents of the Tremé, who also shared stories of attending altars in the homes of their Sicilian neighbors. I asked them why the Black Masking Indians came out on St. Joseph's Night, and we agreed that they dressed and paraded in conjunction with the altars to say thank you and perhaps as a sign of solidarity between two marginalized communities.

That night, when the Indians took to the streets, the New Orleans Police Department clashed with them. The incident exposed not only inequalities in the treatment of many native New Orleanians but also that some local traditions were under attack. Following the incident, Big Chief Allison "Tootie" Montana of the Yellow Pocahontas, who had visited the altar earlier that day, demanded a meeting with the City Council. Tragically, Chief Montana suffered a fatal heart attack while addressing the City Council at that special meeting in June. Just two months after his death, Hurricane Katrina hit the city, and the following day, the levees failed, flooding the city and killing an estimated 1,300 people. Buildings could be rebuilt, but the culture and the people who created the city could not. It was a time of desperation, both physical and spiritual.

That fateful day I spent with Father LeDoux and all the neighbors prompted my years of research into St. Joseph's Day. Father LeDoux loved history and had written a book about St. Augustine Church. He encouraged my curiosity about people and history, asking me to help sort through boxes of old files stored in the church office. Perhaps he recognized our shared love of history.

After Katrina, my sister and I shuttered our thirteen-year-old mask shop in the French Quarter. I attended culinary school but soon realized that as much as I loved food and cooking, research interested me more. In 2016, I began pursuing my master of science degree in urban studies at the University of New Orleans. I aimed to explore aspects of Sicilian immigrants' foodways, a topic that had been rarely studied in New Orleans. While researching the history of Sicilians in the city, I came across several advertisements for masked balls held on St. Joseph's Night. I found them fascinating, but I had other topics to study.

A few years later, COVID-19 swept the world, and I suddenly found myself unemployed for the first time. In my free time, I set out to uncover the true history of this mysterious holiday. I had yet to learn just how intricate its patterns and connections were or the complicated reasons for the changes that have taken place in its celebration.

New Orleans is a city defined by its celebrations. Although most people think immediately of Mardi Gras, for me the most exciting holiday is St. Joseph's Day, which is celebrated in New Orleans like nowhere else. Many other countries observe Carnival, which culminates in the grand event of Mardi Gras. However, only in New Orleans do the Black Masking Indians and Sicilians celebrate St. Joseph's Day. The history of this unique Creole holiday has been overlooked. Before it became known solely for altars and Indians, St. Joseph's Day served as a second Mardi Gras for the entire city, but its trajectory was shaped by evolving concepts of race in the city. As Mardi Gras became less transgressive and more mainstream, St. Joseph's Day opened a space where systems of oppression could be challenged, not through mockery but through vibrant expressions of pride, whether in the elaborate altars filled with food or the striking displays of feathered finery.

Many books and exhibits have explored what we know about the holiday today, but its origins remain unclear, as do the connections between the Black Masking Indians and Sicilian altars. What we do know is that St. Joseph's Day served as a conduit connecting people and allowing them to express themselves. My research reveals that the Black Masking Indians costume, or mask, on St. Joseph's Day because of an older folk tradition that is connected to but not part of Catholic celebrations.

In this book, I argue that St. Joseph's Day was originally a more inclusive celebration in New Orleans, characterized by masking and balls inspired by the holiday known as mid-Lent (*mi-Carême* in French). Its popularity declined because of racial implications stemming from the diminishing influence of Creole French Catholics, the city's Americanization, and the rise of Mardi Gras as the quintessential New Orleans holiday. Some festivities persisted in a fragmented manner, eventually evolving into a holiday with two primary celebrants: the Black Masking Indians and Sicilian Americans. It is often assumed that these two groups celebrate the same holiday, when in fact they interpret the day differently—as mid-Lent and as the saint's feast day, respectively. Nonetheless, both groups initially celebrated the holiday to elevate their status through bold displays of ethnic pride intended to be seen and admired.

Because of the lack of information about the origins of traditions surrounding St. Joseph's Day, I have asked various individuals over the years—Black Masking Indians, Sicilian Americans who had built altars, and both seasoned and young scholars—about the history of this holiday. No one has yet offered a meaningful and comprehensive explanation. I believe that the answer to the riddle of St. Joseph's Day in New Orleans is intertwined with the complexities of history.

Nineteenth- and twentieth-century newspaper articles and advertisements, as well as the Federal Writers' Project Papers at the Cammie G. Henry Research Center at Northwestern State University of Louisiana in Natchitoches, have proven to be invaluable resources for uncovering the forgotten history of St. Joseph's Day. Although many New Orleans history books and articles covering the colonial and antebellum periods do mention the holiday, most do little more than state that masked balls were a tradition and that the day marked the end of the social season, without further explanation. A few books allude to the connection between St. Joseph's Day and mid-Lent but do not provide additional details. For instance, in his essential book *Big Chief Harrison and the Mardi Gras Indians,* Al Kennedy notes that the day was one of celebration and signified a break in Lent without explicitly identifying it as mid-Lent.

In *Romantic New Orleanians,* Robert Tallant highlights that St. Joseph's Day marked mid-Lent by noting that a series of masquerade balls, which began on Twelfth Night and continued through Mardi Gras, "were suspended for the first part of Lent, then had their final dance of the year on St. Joseph's Night, or mi-Carême (mid-Lent in French) March 19." *Gumbo Ya-Ya,* a book compiled from research stemming from the Federal Writers' Project, explains that the night was a time for masquerades, suggesting a link between St. Joseph's Day and mid-Lent.

R. Randall Couch discusses St. Joseph's Day in his seminal article, "The Public Masked Balls of Antebellum New Orleans: A Custom of Masque Outside the Mardi Gras Tradition." He includes St. Joseph's Day among the top three days for masked balls in New Orleans and notes that they "had taken place for years" on this day, although he does not provide further explanation. Another book stemming from the Federal Writers' Project, *The WPA Guide to New Orleans,* states that "usually falling near the middle of Lent, it [St. Joseph's Day] is for this reason called Mi-Carême. The feast originated centuries ago among a small group of Italians exiled because of a religious dispute." Thus, this guide presented a completely different origin story while entirely overlooking the masking traditions on that day.

Sicilian St. Joseph's Day is often mistakenly conflated with mid-Lent traditions. My research shows that the Sicilian altars had no connection to earlier masking traditions, except in name and date. In Sicily, St. Joseph's Day is observed as the feast day of St. Joseph and Father's Day, but not as mid-Lent. Early settlement patterns might have contributed to the confusion. Many of the newly arrived immigrants settled in Black neighborhoods, where cross-cultural exchanges took place. Some older Black Masking Indians recall that stops at altars were part of the night's plan.

Conversely, books on later New Orleans history often overlook the importance of masking and masked balls on St. Joseph's Day. Many authors incorrectly connect these St. Joseph's Day festivities to altars created by Sicilian descendants, misrepresenting these two celebrations as linked. Black Masking Indians remain the only feature of St. Joseph's Day that connects it to mid-Lent.

This book also fills many gaps in the city's history. Using the holiday as a framework, a story emerges about the changing racial dynamics within New Orleans over the years, beginning with the colonial masked balls. It charts the growth of Mardi Gras, a holiday now synonymous with the city, both in relation to the origin of St. Joseph's Day and as a catalyst for its decline. This book weaves together the histories of various segments of New Orleans society, each playing a significant role in the narrative of St. Joseph's Day and the city's evolution.

Chapter 1 introduces Catholicism and discusses its influence on the city, the holidays it celebrates, and how a Catholic way of life has shaped what is now known as "Creole." Specifically, it traces St. Joseph's Day from its origins in France to the solemn religious ceremonies in New France (Canada) and its transformation in the colony of Louisiana. I elaborate on the direct connection between New France and explain why mid-Lent became known as St. Joseph's Day—but only in New Orleans. The development of New Orleans Creole culture and its distinctive holiday St. Joseph's Day is detailed, revealing an evolution closely tied to the changing concepts of race in the city.

Chapter 2 explores the colonial Creoles' passion for highly expressive dancing at masked balls, at which the dancers' racial identity was often hidden. It examines the first ballrooms built in New Orleans and the emergence of deep-rooted communal living, as well as a form of civil religion in which survival, rather than race and class, took precedence. It begins with the introduction of masked balls to the French colony, explores the changing celebrations in the city under Spanish rule, and continues up to the Louisiana Purchase, when the arrival of Anglo-Americans posed a threat to the culture of French Creole New Orleans.

Chapter 3 considers the reasons behind the flourishing of balls during early statehood and emphasizes the rise of Creole culture in antebellum New Orleans. The unique connection of St. Joseph's Day with masking led to tensions between old-line Creoles and new Anglo-Americans. The ballrooms that hosted these masked balls became battlegrounds for these conflicts, contributing to the development of the Creole culture that the city is celebrated for today. The content of St. Joseph's Day advertisements challenges the notion that the town was entirely segregated. Balls transformed into spaces where New Orleanians came together and interacted; once divisive, these events evolved into a force that helped sustain Creole culture.

Chapter 4 examines the transformation of cultural life in New Orleans during the Civil War, occupation, Reconstruction, and beyond. Balls, although still a popular source of entertainment, became more stratified and exclusive as the Americanization of Carnival progressed. Masked balls on St. Joseph's Day became venues of exclusion, operated by groups often connected to the remnants of the Confederacy or ethnic associations. Efforts were made to Americanize St. Joseph's Day, but instead, Anglo-Americans chose to organize Mardi Gras to suit their preferences. As Mardi Gras grew in popularity, it became synonymous with New Orleans, and in response, the popularity of St. Joseph's Day began to decline, taking on a more ethnic character.

Chapter 5 exposes St. Joseph's Night as a more fragmented holiday, no longer shared by all residents. The street celebrations of Black New Orleanians may have existed earlier, but they thrived after the era of the grand, formal masked balls. As private places became the realm of the wealthy, white elite, public spaces were transformed by marginalized people into places of resistance. These alternative festivities became the domain not only of Black Masking Indians but also of many other groups that took to the streets, including the Baby Dolls and previously overlooked groups such as the Western Girls.

Chapter 6 spotlights the altars created by locals of Sicilian descent on St. Joseph's Day, along with the surprising story of their earlier celebrations in New Orleans, which honored the saint's feast day with street processions and public gatherings, rather than the private home altars that proliferated throughout the early twentieth century. Other connections between Black and Sicilian residents are explored through altars in Black Spiritual churches. Today, these altars have morphed from intimate affairs into more public displays of Sicilian ethnic pride. These St. Joseph's Day celebrations have adapted to changing times and have thrived due to the rich, dynamic interactions between Black New Orleanians and the Sicilian families who settled nearby.

My research challenges the long-accepted explanation for the emergence of the Black Masking Indians on St. Joseph's Night. Although the altars and Indian celebrations were not initially connected, they contributed to the popularity and survival of St. Joseph's Day in New Orleans. Both have used the holiday to create spaces that convey history while navigating a hostile world. My new perspective enhances the existing scholarship, addresses a significant gap in New Orleans's history, and demonstrates that much history remains to be discovered.

St. Joseph's Day flourished through the rich and dynamic interaction between Black New Orleanians and the Sicilian families. It was created and continues to exist due to a blend of localization and creolization. Born in France, baptized in New France, and brought to New Orleans—where it was enriched by African and Sicilian rituals—St. Joseph's Day is truly a Creole holiday.

1

CREATING A CREOLE HOLIDAY

Cultural Catholicism Is Established

A chameleon of a word, Creole has, in the most general sense, both masked and exposed anxieties over place, culture, and race.

—SHIRLEY ELIZABETH THOMPSON, *Exiles at Home: The Struggle to Become American in Creole New Orleans*

Adaptability was the essence of becoming Creole.

—LAWRENCE POWELL, *The Accidental City*

In 2010, Vincent Marcello, a resident of the French Quarter, decided to build a swimming pool in his yard on North Rampart Street. He recalled that in 1984, a neighboring property owned by a cousin had uncovered colonial remains, as this block was once the site of the city's oldest graveyard, the St. Peter Street Cemetery. He contacted Dr. Ryan Gray, who conducted a test dig. At a depth of four feet, he uncovered cypress wood, which led him to suspect he had found a coffin; remains were indeed discovered on the property, prompting an archaeological excavation. These new finds prompted archaeologists to revisit artifacts from the earlier dig, including a long silver necklace, possibly a rosary made of sixty-three black wooden beads, and a long wooden cross inlaid with a "fine silver plated chain" adorned with three charms and two double-sided Roman Catholic medals featuring four different saints. This amulet was found with the remains of a man, likely of African descent, who was buried in 1775. Initially, one of the images of these saints was thought to be St. Anthony, but on further examination in 2011, it became clear that it was actually St. Joseph.[1]

From New Orleans's beginnings, St. Joseph was a beloved saint, so much so that the city's residents merged his feast day with the secular holiday of mid-Lent—providing a brief reprieve from the forty days of prayer and fasting observed in remembrance of Jesus's suffering before his resurrection on Easter Sunday. Since St. Joseph's Day is celebrated on the same day every year during Lent—March 19—it gave French Catholic settlers in New Orleans a consistent opportunity to incorporate an Old World tradition into their new lives. To understand the evolution of St. Joseph's Day in New Orleans requires an examination of its impact on Catholicism, Creolization, and race relations. It is the story of how the saint's feast day made its way to New Orleans and how local attitudes toward race influenced the celebration of St. Joseph's Day.

Joseph, the husband of Mary and the foster father of Jesus Christ, is scarcely mentioned in the New Testament. Nor did his image appear in Christian art of the Nativity until the fifth century CE, and this was probably intentional: his exclusion enabled the Catholic Church to direct congregations toward the divinity of Jesus and to weaken doubts about his Virgin birth. Over time, church tradition focused on the Holy Family as a model of devotion. Joseph embodied someone everyone could identify with, providing a way for ordinary people to connect with their faith. Because little was documented about him, the opportunities for interpretation were extensive. He became the patron saint of the universal church, families, fathers, workers, home sellers, carpenters, a good death, and, eventually, New France.

Roman Catholicism was the state religion in France and its colonies. Shortly after Samuel de Champlain established New France in present-day Canada, Franciscan missionaries declared Joseph the patron saint of the colony.[2] Father Joseph Le Caron, a French Récollet and one of four founding priests of Québec, invoked this dedication in this 1624 prayer: "We have since that time had a great solemnity, when all the settlers were present and many Indians, for a vow we have made to St. Joseph, whom we have chosen Patron of the country and protector of this rising church."[3]

The Récollets and the Jesuits, Catholic missionaries in New France, developed a devotion to St. Joseph, as evidenced by the numerous instances of his name found throughout the new colony. Father Paul Le Jeune, a Jesuit who worked in New France from 1632 to 1639, recounted the events that occurred on St. Joseph's Eve in the budding colony of Québec on March 18, 1637: "On the eve of this day which is so dear to us, the flag was hoisted and the cannon fired, as I have said above. Monsieur the Governor had an exhibition of fireworks, as artistically devised as almost any I had seen in France; on one side a skin was stretched, upon which appeared in illuminated letters the name of St. Joseph; above this sacred name burned a number of lighted candles from which sprang eighteen or twenty little serpents." The priest remarked that on the next day, the feast of St. Joseph, the church was nearly as full as it was on Easter, one of the holiest days on the liturgical calendar.[4]

A decade or so later, on St. Joseph's Eve in 1649, the Hurons, close allies of the French, were attacked by the Iroquois, their fiercest rivals in the fur trade. Jesuit priest Paul Ragueneau, head of the Huron mission and an eyewitness to the attack, decided that "help could only come from heaven" and vowed to celebrate a mass in honor of St. Joseph each month for a year if he survived. Many in his group made similar personal vows, hoping for a miracle to save them. That day passed in silence; on the next day, March 19, the "day of the great St. Joseph, a sudden panic fell upon the enemy camp," and the Iroquois soon retreated.[5]

In 1667, René-Robert Cavelier, Sieur de La Salle, born in Rouen and educated by the Jesuits, arrived in New France. He sailed down the Mississippi River in 1682, claiming it and the entire region for France and naming it La Louisiane in honor of King Louis XIV.[6] Accompanying the explorer was Father Zénobe (or Zenobius) Membré, a Récollet priest, tasked with transplanting Catholicism to La Louisiane and offering the first prayer over the new territory.[7] La Salle preferred the Récollet priests to the Jesuits because he believed the latter were interested in complete control not only of religious instruction but also of the fur trade. Before he returned home that year, Father Zénobe blessed the cross that La Salle had erected to claim possession of the territory for Catholic France.[8] In 1724, Catholicism was established as the official religion of Louisiana, and St. Joseph became linked to the area.

Many of the original settlers were *coureurs de bois,* meaning "wood runners." Their origins are often linked to Samuel de Champlain, who, in 1627, allegedly brought young French boys to live among Indigenous peoples near the colonized areas. These boys were tasked with learning Native languages and customs to improve communication and expand trade. Early French colonizers also tried to impose their culture on the Native peoples by encouraging them to convert to Catholicism and by introducing European trade goods like guns, beads, and textiles. As settlers made contact, established trade, and sometimes formed kinship ties with Indigenous peoples, this shift was driven by their dual goals of gaining land and ensuring survival: coureurs de bois were traders, not farmers, relying on food and shelter from Indigenous communities. Their livelihoods in the fur trade depended heavily on that support.

Later, the Jesuits, favored over the Récollets by Pierre Le Moyne d'Iberville, recognized that conversion depended on the Native peoples' assimilation, believing they should "learn their languages and integrate Christianity into their way of life rather than force them to become French."[9] In the colonies of New France, many Frenchmen formed familial ties with Indigenous women—whether through coercion or willingly—leading to a more relaxed understanding of race. This attitude toward multicultural mixing carried over to the territory of Louisiana, where such openness to mingling, among other factors, would later influence the lifestyle of New Orleans residents. As a result, these coureurs de bois were "transformed from renegades and outlaws into agents for cultural assimilation in the new colony of Louisiana."[10] Thanks to this "openness to peoples of other races and cultures," settlers in New Orleans not only survived but also thrived; local Native Americans played a crucial role in their survival during the early years of the first French era.[11]

New Orleans eventually emerged as a frontier town in the Louisiana colony while maintaining its connections with New France, solidifying St. Joseph's importance across French North America. In 1699, the first eighty Louisiana settlers were primarily men from New France; they included French naval officers and soldiers, as well as artisans from the motherland. By 1719, 28 women and 196 men were in the region.[12] Although colonial New Orleans was French, the early colonists created a community steeped in an "extension of the French experience in Canada."[13] Lawrence N. Powell refers to this community as a "hybrid culture," possibly building on George Washington Cable's idea of New Orleans as a "hybrid city" in Cable's book set in the early 1800s. St. Joseph's Day and its evolution embodied Powell's idea that the "creation of a hybrid culture—a Creole culture, whose whole was always more significant than the sum of its ethnic parts—is one of the Atlantic World's most vital contributions to modernity. It was never the result of 'borrowing' an African retention here, a European tradition there, so much as the product of 'creating' or 'remodeling.'"[14] According to Darryl Barthé, "the origins of Louisiana and of the Creole peoples of Louisiana [were] in Quebec."[15] French Catholic homogeneity combined with the wildness of the Americas to lay the groundwork for the Creole identity of New Orleans and the laissez-faire attitude for which the area would become famous.

Colonial New Orleanians first identified as Creole because they were born in Louisiana, spoke French, and practiced Catholicism regardless of race. Over time, dynamic Creole cultural pluralism became the central "religion," and the city that emerged was culturally Catholic.[16] Being "Creole" was always ambiguous because "assimilation of a new culture is always partial and fragmentary," which inspired adjustments over the years in New Orleans to fluctuations in immigration, disease, hunger, and commercial output.[17] Yet, everything associated with the city—holidays like St. Joseph's Day, music, food, and even plants—would become Creolized. New Orleans Creoles sought to follow in the footsteps of their Canadian forefathers by "seeking to create their own New World social order and identity."[18]

The Catholic Church's response to dealing with issues of race was complex. During the colonial era, the enslaved—both Native Americans and those captured from Africa—were encouraged or forced to attend Catholic churches and participate in rituals such as baptism, leading to cultural genocide. However, because of "the benign neglect of the crown, the colony was quickly becoming a métis [having mixed Indigenous and European ancestry] colony, in fact, and in reputation, the population rapidly becoming a racial mixture of French, Native Americans, and Africans."[19] These bonds of religion, language, culture, and shared values led to high rates of interracial relationships and a lax interpretation of race, a phenomenon rarely seen in the colonial world and leading directly to the emergence of New Orleans Creole. During the late 1700s, relationships formed that were "culturally endogamous even if they may have been perceived as racially exogamous."[20]

According to Canadian historian W. J. Eccles, a general lack of religious enthusiasm and a chronic shortage of clergy and funds made it virtually impossible for the church in Louisiana to launch the same sort of missionary drive that had been waged in the preceding century in New France in Canada. As a result, miscegenation between white men and Black or Indigenous women, which the Catholic Church officially opposed, persisted through Spanish rule and until the Louisiana Purchase, regardless of its illegality. Thus, Catholicism laid the foundation for colonial life in Louisiana but in many ways became Creolized along the way.

More liberal rules and intermarriage persisted after the arrival of new "settlers" to the colony, a group of unsavory characters from Paris. In 1717, condemned male prisoners were offered reduced sentences if they cleared and cultivated land in Louisiana; after doing so for three years, they were promised ownership of some of the land they had worked.[21] Imprisoned females were promised their freedom if they came to the colony. In 1720, the ship *La Mutine* arrived with two hundred women, all convicted criminals. However, as Joan DeJean recently discovered, many had been questionably accused and seemed to be victims of poverty, rather than brutal criminals.[22] In any event, these ragtag residents had little reason to concern themselves with race because most were trying to forge a new existence with little resources.

In addition, white men greatly outnumbered white women in the colony. Because white women were so rare, they were treated like commodities, imported and practically sold from the docks as wives. During the early years of the colony, interracial marriage—whether between white men and Native American women or white men and Black women—was almost inevitable, which led to a casual acceptance of mixed-race residents.

In 1722, the Capuchins arrived in Louisiana, expanding the Catholic influence established by the Jesuits.[23] Their belief in the equality of all Catholics, regardless of race or class, would revolutionize the New Orleans church by fostering a relative inclusiveness and tolerance.[24] The Catholic hierarchy was more liberal than the extremely conservative French officials and "though more assertive than the Protestant church, left much room for cultural adaptations and syncretism." Catholicism figured heavily in the cultural formation of New Orleans; many of its celebrations formed the foundation of a civil religion that became more secular over time.[25] Dianne Guenin-Lelle argues that the Catholic church not only disseminated spiritual beliefs but also served as an organizing force in all aspects of life, including holidays.[26]

In colonial Louisiana, "red, white, and black met under crisis conditions," where constant threats of disease and starvation fostered a culture of mutual dependence.[27] In New Orleans, race was constructed much like the flow of the Mississippi River, which is never still, often turbulent, and sometimes shifted by barriers. The city's makeup contributed to a complex perspective on racism, although religious fervor, slavery, and racism continued to be challenges endemic to the New World and to New Orleans.

In 1769, under Spanish rule, the enslavement of Indigenous peoples was deemed illegal, leading to manumissions not only for Indigenous people but also for some enslaved Africans who disputed their heritage. The Spanish also brought the custom of *coartación,* or the right to pay one's way out of enslavement.[28] Even though freedom was more accessible to a few, this did not mean that slavery in New Orleans and the surrounding area was any less brutal than in non-Spanish colonies; many Indigenous people were systematically denied their freedom. The fact remained that slavery as an institution was never questioned. Indigenous people often were held captive and designated as being of African descent to keep them enslaved. Many were denied freedom because the Spanish governor, Francisco Luis Héctor de Carondelet, worried that freeing too many enslaved Indigenous people would ruin many families financially.[29] The Spanish and, later, the Americans were also concerned about the growing number of free people of color. By the late 1700s, some enslaved and free Black Creoles began negotiating their racial standing by declaring themselves and family members as Indigenous, rather than Black, accelerating the move toward a biracial, more rigid hierarchy.[30]

For example, in 1799, Clara López de la Peña from New Orleans wrote to the archdiocese requesting that her daughter Luisa's racial classification on her baptismal record be changed from "negro" to "white," citing her mother's Indigenous ancestry and her father being of European stock. To support her request, she gathered numerous documents and listed individuals who vouched for her mestiza status as the daughter of a Native American and a European.[31] Clara understood that the stigma of Blackness would be detrimental to her daughter's future, but she also recognized that the concept of whiteness was not yet fixed in New Orleans. Clara succeeded, and her daughter's name was transferred from the book of "negroes" to the book of "whites."

Catholic influence persisted during Spanish rule, as Spanish Capuchins succeeded French Capuchins. Antonio de Sedella, affectionately known to French-speaking New Orleanians as Père Antoine, was a popular Spanish priest who both respected and inserted himself into the existing French culture. In 1786, twenty years after the colony's transfer to Spanish authority, Père Antoine sought permission for three French nuns to reside at the Ursuline convent. Letters from the archdiocesan archives show the surprise expressed by the Diocese of Cuba that Sedella allowed the French nuns to "reside in the convent of the Ursulines where they will disturb the peace of the Spanish nuns."[32] Even after two decades of Spanish governance, the bond between France and the city residents seemed to remain strong as New Orleanians clung to their Gallic language and culture.

On October 20, 1792, Father Portillo, a priest in New Orleans, expressed shame and regret about his own poor French pronunciation after a fellow priest, Father Luis, was reassigned following an incident in Pointe Coupée Parish in which "the ridicule excited" by his sermons got out of hand.[33] Clearly, the people of Louisiana fought to preserve their Frenchness, even if it meant mocking a man of the cloth.

French Catholicism played a significant role in forging a shared identity between Black and white residents, contributing to the growth of the population segment known as *gens de couleur libres,* or free people of color. In addition, from its earliest years in New Orleans, the Catholic Church expected both enslaved and free people of color to worship and receive sacraments. In doing so, the church and the colony welcomed people of color into their religion and, eventually, into society. In 1724, the twenty-third recorded marriage in the colony was between two free people of color. French-styled Catholicism, practiced by Black New Orleanians, provided "a degree of cultural continuity for the second and third generations of French, Spanish, African, and West Indian settlers as the territory transitioned from French and Spanish to American hands."[34] The period of French ideals and later weak Spanish control set the stage for a new era when the Republic of the United States acquired New Orleans by purchasing the Louisiana Territory in 1803. Soon thereafter, the concept of Creole would be called into question.

Depending on the circumstances and time, the term "Creole" in Louisiana has referred to individuals of European descent, of mixed race, and of Black descent with French and Spanish ancestry born in Louisiana. Consequently, the designation has been fraught with confusion and contention. However, after the Louisiana Purchase, the term "Creole" came to be used to distinguish between those born in Louisiana and new Anglo-American residents.[35] The latter believed that "being Creole signaled the likelihood of racial mixture"; this characterization reinforced their biracial hierarchical system.[36] As they questioned the "whiteness" of anyone identifying as Creole, many white Creoles feared the repercussions of such an association, and many dropped identifying as such. Today, some believe that Creole is a racial designation, but it is not.

Alongside Creole culture, which many Anglo-Americans found perplexing, Catholicism and its associated holidays significantly influenced the perception of New Orleans as a "foreign city." The city's development, shaped by religious teachings, attitudes, and social customs, distinguished it from the rest of the country. From the beginning, New Orleans was predominantly Catholic—not always in practice but certainly in governance and celebration. Unlike the original thirteen states, its founding was closely tied to the Roman Catholic Church. Although Louisiana was acquired early in the nation's history, the founding fathers soon recognized that the territory lacked the "triumph of Protestantism or the excellence of reason."[37] Consequently, its Catholicism was quickly understood as one of the reasons why it would prove so challenging to Americanize the local citizens. Indeed, New Orleanians did not shrink from but embraced the city's unique characteristics.

The Haitian Revolution, which began in 1791, increased the influence of France, the Catholic Church, and the free people of color, much to the dismay of the new Anglo-American leadership. The French Catholic refugees, who fled the revolution in Saint-Domingue (later known as Haiti) and stayed briefly in Cuba and Jamaica, doubled New Orleans's population: two-thirds of these refugees were enslaved individuals or free people of color. They "served to augment the church in New Orleans, and people of color were generous in their support."[38]

The shared French language, similar celebrations, and Catholicism continued to connect New Orleanians, but racial divisions began to deepen over time. After the Louisiana Purchase, it became clear that free people of color were not being guaranteed the "rights of full citizenship" under American rule, widening the chasm.[39] Even so, white Creoles worried that their established rights would be at risk. They attempted to distinguish themselves from Creoles of color but, at the same time, relied on them to uphold their French cultural traditions, which led to further conflict with the new US administration.

The founding fathers believed that American settlement in the area would speed up the Americanization of New Orleanians, but much to President Jefferson's surprise, the opposite occurred: many Anglos new to the area assimilated into Creole ways after marrying into local families.[40] The Louisiana Purchase did not slow the growth of Creole culture in New Orleans. Catholic-related celebrations were the norm, and to fit in socially, the new Anglo-Americans eventually adopted holidays such as St. Joseph's Day and Mardi Gras.

Dancing, a significant cultural marker in New Orleans, was actually promoted by the Catholic Church, particularly the Jesuits, who used dance and spectacle to "attract and inspire believers."[41] Many early Catholic missionaries viewed Native American dances and feasts as opportunities for conversion, comparing the Indigenous peoples' appreciation for spectacle and respect for ritual to the grandeur of French Catholicism; thus, dancing was never forbidden.[42]

From the beginning, New Orleanians rarely missed an opportunity to engage in festivities, often displaying a unique irreverence influenced by French culture. As Samuel Kinser points out, in New Orleans, "man's right to relaxation was spelled with a French accent." This same French influence was responsible for the signature holiday of New Orleans, Mardi Gras. Its name means Fat Tuesday: it is the final day of Carnival and of the festive season before Lent begins. During Lent, there is another quasi-religious holiday, mid-Lent. Mid-Lent is usually celebrated on the fourth Sunday or the Thursday of the third week of Lent, a movable feast day that changes each year to align with the date of Easter. In New Orleans, it came to be celebrated each year on March 19 and to be referred to as St. Joseph's Day. Both Mardi Gras and mid-Lent are responses to the austerity of Lent's religious fervor, either to prepare for or to alleviate the accompanying suffering.

Colonial records indicate that leniency during Lent was common in New Orleans. In the 1790s, the New Orleans archdiocese specified that oils and fats, eggs, and dairy products were allowed during Lent but not for how long nor under what conditions.[43] Because New Orleans is surrounded by water rich in seafood, restrictions on eating meat were not necessarily seen as a sacrifice. As a prelate visiting the city in 1940, 150 years or so later, pointed out after enjoying a seafood feast, "Abstinence of meat on Friday certainly should not be penance. It would be one indeed were it reversed, and seafood denied."[44]

During Lent, the church also discouraged sexual intercourse and only allowed marriages that had been granted special permission.[45] Joan DeJean, when discussing marriages following the November 29, 1729, Natchez Massacre, notes that those who were widowed had already remarried by early 1730. However, after one wedding on February 20, 1730, "there was a lull during which no new ceremonies were performed until April 12."[46] Given that Easter that year was on April 9, it seems reasonable to conclude that weddings were not performed because of Lent.

However, many marriages were later conducted on mid-Lent in New Orleans. As late as 1907, "wedding bells rang merrily, for it was St. Joseph's Night." More than seventy-five couples from all walks of life were married that night. Board of Health records indicate that most marriage licenses requested in March specified the date as either St. Joseph's Eve or Night, proving that St. Joseph's Day and mid-Lent in New Orleans were the same.[47] In 1891, one local newspaper noted that "a joyful event like marriage" was not compatible with the "penitential season of Lent" and urged that marriages should be postponed until after Easter. "Some superstitious persons imagine that St. Joseph's Day, which falls during Lent, is the best day of the year to marry." However, the article concludes, "Surely, St. Joseph will not bless these superstitious persons, who do not heed the commands and wishes of the church."[48] Enforcing the idea of St. Joseph's Day as mid-Lent was not sanctioned by the Catholic church.

In his book *The Mistick Krewe: Chronicles of Comus and His Kin,* Perry Young explains the connection between Mardi Gras and mid-Lent. In France, during the Middle Ages, the young men in the village gave "a final masquerade ball for the maidens on the night of Mardi Gras, and at mi-carême [mid-Lent] the girls returned the courtesy." The young women organized this final masquerade of the year to thank the young men for the party on Mardi Gras.[49]

St. Joseph's Night also sparked other festivities in New Orleans, because it was the one time during Lent when New Orleanians' favorite pastime—

dancing in costume—was allowed, making masked balls inevitable then. According to Robert Tallant, celebrations on St. Joseph's Day originated with masked balls directly related to mid-Lent:

> Perhaps the most ancient of those balls connected with Mardi Gras were the famed *Bals du Roi,* or King's Balls, which took place on Twelfth-Night, January 6. At a ball, or even a family dinner, a king cake, sometimes called a twelfth-cake, was cut, and the finder of the bean was the host or hostess of the next great celebration. This was a custom that began in the earliest days of New Orleans. The finding of the bean began a series of balls, almost all of them masquerades that lasted until Shrove Tuesday or Mardi Gras, were suspended for the first part of Lent, then had their final dance of the year on St. Joseph's Night, or mi-careme, March 19.[50]

Traditionally, in New Orleans, mid-Lent was not only the day Catholics took a break from the rigors of abstinence during Lent but also marked the official end of the season of masked balls: it thereby extended the Carnival season into one last day during Lent. St. Joseph's Day thus became another "traditional excuse for a spate of balls."[51]

Eventually, mid-Lent balls and festivities became associated with the lower classes both in New Orleans and France. In Gustave Flaubert's 1856 novel *Madame Bovary,* the final week of Emma's life and her descent into hell begin at a mi-Carême costume ball. Earlier in the book, she attends another masked ball, which is described as an elegant and beautiful affair. In contrast, the mi-Carême ball is portrayed as filled with rowdy commoners who are drunk and unruly. Flaubert characterizes mi-Carême festivities as "frivolous celebrations" that are "vestiges of earlier pagan celebrations."[52] Whether mid-Lent was related to pagan fêtes is not important; what is key is that it had already been marginalized in France by the time of *Madame Bovary*'s publication in 1856.

In France, mi-Carême celebrations would continue but became connected to the day of "La Reine des Reines" (Queen of Queens), alluding to the parade and ball of the most beautiful washerwoman in Paris. When

George Sala visited Paris in 1893, he remarked that mi-Carême had "degenerated into an offensive pageant" with "showily attired washer-women." It is not known when mid-Lent became the holiday of the laundresses; perhaps the holiday lost respectability because of their participation.

By the 1920s, mi-Carême entered the realm of the rebellious underworld of Paris, characterized by student protests and lively masked balls such as the one at the Magic-City on Quai d'Orsay, which enjoyed strong gay support. It featured drag queens until 1935; after that, they were no longer permitted because the balls had to "be in good taste."[53]

In New Orleans, St. Joseph's Day remained a major source of entertainment for a wider audience over a longer period, perhaps because the city fully embraced its reputation as a wicked place where anything goes. In the early 1800s, Timothy Flint, a Protestant American from Massachusetts, shared his first impression of the city, which included this memorable description:

> Much has been said about the profligacy of manners, and morals here; and this place has more than once been called the modern Sodom. Amidst such a multitude, composed in a great measure of the low people of all nations, there must of course be much debauchery, and low vice. Where it appears in this form, it is so disgusting, and the tippling houses, and other resorts of vice, have such an aspect of beastliness and degradation, as to render them utterly *unbearable.*

He also pointed out that there "are many excellent people here, many people who mourn over the prevailing degeneracy. Among the Protestants, when I was there, were many unions for religious purposes, female religious societies, efforts to build a mariners' church, a Bethel flag flying, and apparently much excitement of religious feeling."[54]

Flint suggested that the Catholic Church had either tolerated such behavior or was the source of these questionable habits and that Protestantism provided a solution to the city's problems. Nonetheless, the influence of French Catholicism remained strong in New Orleans throughout the antebellum period and into the Civil War. During this time, St. Joseph's Day celebrations flourished as the city grew alongside the holiday.

A more segregated society emerged around the same time. The struggle to align Creole culture with whiteness began before the Civil War, when racial tensions ran high. Numerous factors led the new Anglo-American residents to question the cultural practices of the old-line white Creoles. "Public social proximity and even overt intimacy with people of color could not be separated in the Anglo public imagination from their ethnic-cultural identity as Creoles."[55] Indeed, "there was undoubtedly more intimacy between the races in New Orleans than in most Southern states which, only a decade after the Civil War, permitted interracial marriages, and which outlawed segregation in schools and places of public accommodation."[56]

Creole identity became a liability to white New Orleanians as Anglo-American power grew. To avoid having their racial purity questioned, most white Creoles abandoned the moniker, but French Creole celebrations persisted amidst the confusion of race and ethnicity.[57] Catholic celebrations and holidays like St. Joseph's Day defined Creole as much as anything else. The balls offered a glimpse into a somewhat inclusive celebration that gradually transformed to reflect the city's changing culture of race relations.

In Union-controlled New Orleans, no Catholic churches were closed, although at least forty Protestant ones were shuttered. The Catholic churches likely remained open because they did not offer prayers for the Confederate soldiers: "Eighteen centuries of experience had taught the Catholic hierarchy how to behave in the presence of a conqueror."[58]

During Reconstruction, Catholic administrators wisely kept the churches open to everyone; physical segregation would come later. Their neutral stance during this period supported the church's growth because it "continued to be the spiritual home of almost all Louisianians of Latin descent, all Irish and many Germans." It later included Sicilians who arrived as a source of cheap labor after the enslaved were emancipated; the new immigrants brought with them their twist on St. Joseph's Day. For many

Catholics in New Orleans, racial mixing was still of less concern than the possibility of marriage between Catholics and Protestants or, worse yet, that their children might not attend parochial school.[59]

By the mid-twentieth century, St. Joseph's Day shed its attachment to mid-Lent, and celebrations became more closely associated with the saint's feast day, spurred by the arrival of immigrants from Sicily. New Orleans had emerged as the top destination for Sicilian immigrants fleeing political troubles and devastating harvests. With them, they brought a stronger influence of Latin Catholicism and a new take on St. Joseph's Day, featuring altars and a more sacred celebration honoring St. Joseph as the patron saint of Sicily. In the late 1930s, however, "masquerades and dances still take place in New Orleans and its vicinity that night. Many clubs give parties, and most of the St. Joseph's altar-donors terminate the night in dancing."[60]

Over the years, St. Joseph's Day's celebrations became increasingly segregated. Resistance to racial mixing prompted residents to embrace the biracial culture of the era. White Anglo-Americans gained control of the most popular French Catholic celebration, Mardi Gras, leading to a decline in the popularity of St. Joseph's Day.

Yet Creole culture owes much to both Black and white residents who initiated the celebrations on St. Joseph's Day. The earlier festivities centered on masking for those who continued to recognize the established practices. This tradition survives solely because Black Masking Indians inherited it as a day of costuming and celebration. Later, immigrants from Sicily, who honored the saint with altars on his feast day, added to the commemoration of the day. St. Joseph's Day exemplifies the concept that Creole is both a product of blending and an assertion of identity. Creole offers a chance for individual expression of certain facets of the community, as a whole and as a part.

2

COLONIAL CELEBRATIONS

Setting the Stage for Dancing and Masked Balls on St. Joseph's Day

The Creoles' lone pleasure and dissipation, the male is tirelessly hunting; and both sexes throughout the colony have a particular passion for dancing.

—JAMES PITOT

The story of music in New Orleans must begin with dancing.

—HENRY KMEN

Dance was the most popular form of entertainment in colonial New Orleans. The city's love affair with music grew from the Gallic inclination toward dancing, so it is no surprise that most early celebrations in New Orleans started with dance. Music historian Henry Kmen identifies three reasons why dancing was essential to life in early New Orleans. First, it was an inexpensive activity, needing only a fiddler in its basic form. Second, as a multiethnic, multilingual town, New Orleans used dancing to bridge language barriers; it "was the most nearly universal form of social entertainment." Third, the city's French Catholic roots contributed to its popularity because, in contrast to many Protestant religions, dancing was never seen as sinful.[1] And during much of the colonial era, New Orleans had a "frontier society economy," meaning settlers did little agricultural work. Thus, early rising was not necessary, which made nighttime entertainment, such as balls, more appealing.[2] Later, as the city and its surrounding areas became increasingly reliant on slave-driven agriculture, a leisure culture developed that included dancing and balls.

During King Louis XIV's reign, dance was a vital cultural artifact in France and became more prominent there than in any other Western empire.[3] This passion easily spread to the new colonies, especially Louisiana. The history of the earliest dances, or balls, is intertwined with the city's broader narrative. Initially, these dances were likely private and held on a small scale. New Orleans remained socially and culturally French throughout the colonial years, and the city's celebrations were seen as imitations of those in Paris. However, they existed as a "colonial fragment," lacking many of the rules of class and social structure found in France at the time.[4] Recollections of the celebrations during the first hundred years of New Orleans's history are sparse. However, a decree from Louis XIV "permitting Carnival madness" suggests that celebrations existed and likely included masked balls.[5]

In 1730, Frenchman Marc-Antoine Caillot complained, "We were already quite far along in the Carnival season without having had the least bit of fun or entertainment, which made me miss France a great deal." On Lundi Gras, he expected there to be some celebrations in the city but only found his "associates, who were bored to death." However, there was a strong likelihood that there would be parties in private homes and along the riverfront. And then Caillot remembered that he had been invited to a wedding on Bayou St. John and decided to gather a group of maskers to crash the party together. He persuaded his landlord and wife, who had the proper attire, to join him and head to the bayou. Fortuitously, they encountered along the way a few musicians willing to join the celebration. Marc-Antoine was dressed as "a shepherdess in white," complete with "a corset of white dimity, a muslin skirt, a large pannier, right down to the chemise, along with plenty of beauty marks too." He brought along his "husband, who was the Marquis de Carnival," who was guided by "eight actual Negro slaves, who each carried a flambeau."[6]

Costuming, including cross-dressing, was as acceptable in New Orleans during the colonial era as it is today. During the antebellum era, John H. B. Latrobe, the son of the architect Benjamin Latrobe, described the "handsomest person, male or female," at a ball he attended in 1834 was a man dressed as a woman, whose real identity was not discovered until later in the evening. Latrobe observed many men making "love to him as a female," but he noticed her spitting on the floor, raising his doubts about the person's sex.[7]

During the sixteenth century in France and influenced by Catherine de' Medici, the Italian-born queen, Catholic processions often transformed into vibrant masquerades, with many attendees dressing *in travesti.* French monarchs reinterpreted Catholicism through theater, art, and classical forms of ancient paganism, which helped ease societal tensions and suppress dissenting views by offering holidays as a break from daily life. Instead of banning pagan celebrations, Catholic authorities integrated them into the religious calendar to promote and legitimize the worship of Jesus as the son of God and the veneration of the saints.

Reflecting Parisians' love for costuming and flamboyant dress, New Orleans attracted those who engaged in the "luxury trades." By 1721, with a population of just 470, the city had a wigmaker, three tailors, and a sommelier who managed not just wine but also linens and china of the household; they all worked in the same grand home.[8] A young Ursuline novice, Marie Hachard, remarked that "there is as much politeness and magnificence here as in France, and the use of cloth of gold and velvet is very common, even though it is three times as expensive here as in Rouen." She later noted that the local women would rather live on gruel than give up their dresses made of these sumptuous fabrics, again pointing out their high cost compared to those in France.[9]

Although New Orleanians clamored for luxury items, their behavior was not always as refined as their choice of fabrics: balls in the young community were "known not only for routine rowdyism but for occasional murders." Furthermore, "ballgoers were not always well-versed in the social graces."[10] Balls were such a popular form of entertainment that they attracted people from many places, who came to New Orleans via its busy port. Very little could be done to curb the early colonists' enthusiasm for these events; allegedly, even storms could not deter the fun. The *banquettes,* or wooden sidewalks, would often wash away during the city's frequent deluges, leading residents to walk barefoot to ballrooms, accompanied by the enslaved "carrying their stockings, shoes, a pail of water, and towels." On arrival, "they would repair to a room for that purpose, have the slaves wash and wipe their feet, and after putting on their shoes and stockings or socks, would attend the ball."[11]

In 1743, a new governor from Quebec, Pierre Rigaud, Marquis de Vaudreuil-Cavagnial, arrived with the ambition of introducing refinement to the town. New Orleanians were thrilled that he was a nobleman who established a small-scale royal court mirroring the one in Paris: it presented not only French sophistication to these luxury-loving residents but also BéBé, a Parisian dancing master, who aimed to "teach the children of the next generation how to behave at the most important of occasions, the *soirée dansante,* or ball." Along with New Orleanians' lack of decorum, the inhabitants were viewed as downright unprincipled; as early as 1728, New Orleans had already been labeled a place of questionable morals where, as Marie Hachard discovered, "not only do debauchery, lack of faith and all other vices reign here more than anywhere else, but they reign with an immeasurable abundance!"[12] For a young woman studying to become a nun, much of what she witnessed was shocking, and although not explicitly stated, dancing without regard to class and race was likely part of the debauchery she referenced.

Vaudreuil ignited a new fascination with masked balls.[13] Masking had played a vital role in peasant life under harsh feudal rule in France.[14] It served a similar role in New Orleans, making masking holidays particularly popular as an escape from the grim realities of colonial life, where disease and famine were ever present. Early colonial life in New Orleans was marked by a continuous struggle to survive, leading to "society functioning as a very rudimentary social collective" because everyone relied on one another for survival. And so, in the colony, everyone danced. Even enslaved people were allowed to gather and dance on Sundays, unlike in the British and Spanish colonies of the time; enslaved people living in New Orleans could move around more freely and anonymously than those on plantations, fostering a richer social life as they found ways to meet at night in the gardens hidden behind many homes. Encounters like these were less contentious than in public balls, where everyone mingled—rich and poor, Black and white, free and enslaved.[15] The absence of segregation by class or race helped nurture the emerging Creole culture.

In New Orleans, the enslaved occasionally held balls in their owners' homes that featured dancing, music, food, and drink.[16] Even though enslaved people were often brutalized, these more relaxed rules produced one of the most racially flexible societies in the Americas. The popularity of dancing contributed to this dynamic and later helped foster the vibrant social life of free people of color, an emerging demographic in New Orleans.[17] As Gwendolyn Midlo Hall explains, the colonial period in New Orleans reflected "a heritage and tradition of official corruption, defiance of authority by the poor of all races, and a violence, as well as a brutal, racist tradition that its ruling groups viewed as the only means of containing its competent, well-organized, self-confident, and defiant Afro-Creole population; but it also left behind a tradition of racial openness that could never be entirely repressed."[18]

French colonial Louisiana lacked clear standards to differentiate race, primarily using the term *libre* to distinguish free individuals from enslaved ones. Priests maintained two records, one for Black individuals and another for white individuals, to document baptisms and marriages. However, many people were recorded in the book for white residents, regardless of color.[19] Free people of color were recognized by the city as early as 1722, and evidence of interracial marriages existed by 1732. By that time, "free Negroes" were also counted in the census.[20]

During the 1720s, many enslaved individuals arrived in Louisiana from the west coast of Africa. They included members of the Bambara tribe, who were known for their military expertise. A Black militia was established in Louisiana to serve as a buffer against hostile Native tribes and to help capture escaped slaves, or maroons, living in settlements near New Orleans. This militia later assisted in policing the city and its surrounding areas during both wartime and peacetime. In recognition of their contributions, some Black militiamen were freed and given nearby land to farm. By 1740, a permanent free Black militia was established, leading to significant advancements in their social standing.

In 1762, France ceded Louisiana to Spain in the secret Treaty of Fontainebleau. However, Spain delayed taking control of the territory, which led many residents to believe Louisiana would remain a French colony. Spanish officials, led by Governor Don Antonio de Ulloa, finally arrived in 1766, but Ulloa did not immediately exert control. Because of his concerns about free women of color and their perceived privileges, a law was soon enacted that specifically banned them from wearing masks at dances, yet it was impossible to enforce.[21]

In turn, the colonists had concerns about Ulloa. They complained that he lacked charisma and social skills, that his wife did not participate in Creole social life, including balls, and that the Spanish Capuchin monks "disapproved of the colony's style of worship."[22] The local military even refused to serve under Ulloa or the Spanish flag. In desperation, the local Superior Council, headed by Attorney General Nicolas Chauvin de LaFreniere, a member of the Creole elite, convened on October 29, 1768, to address grievances against Ulloa. The Creole elite wanted the colony to retain their version of Frenchness and for their society, which had been built on French mores, to continue to be supported by slavery and familial ties.

A coup was staged, led by several planters and some residents of the German Coast who were concerned about these and many other issues, including fears that the Spanish would limit trade with France. Ulloa was banished to Spain without any bloodshed—yet. For ten months, the citizens of Louisiana pleaded with France to reclaim the colony, to no avail; having abandoned the colony years earlier, France had no interest in retaking Louisiana. For almost a year, the colony was regarded as "a de facto independent state." Talk of establishing an independent republic persisted. The demoralized New Orleanians believed they had been "placed in a state of liberty through its abandonment by its legitimate owner," but that "the colony held the power to accept or reject the laws prescribed by the new sovereign."

These sentiments were silenced when the second Spanish governor, General Alejandro O'Reilly, appeared in full force in early July 1769. Ultimately, five men, including Attorney General LaFreniere, were accused of treason and sentenced to death by hanging. With no executioner to be found, on October 25, 1769, they were put before a firing squad, and New Orleans became a colony of Spain.[23] However, France and French culture would never be superseded: the city's residents reinvented their Frenchness primarily by retaining French holidays, including social events focused on dancing, which were often masked.

Governor O'Reilly introduced new laws based on the Spanish Las Siete Partidas, or the Seven Divisions, that granted the enslaved more venues to manumission. These rules, the Spanish believed, would diminish the problem of escaped slaves, quell some of the fears of revolts, and increase productivity among the enslaved by enhancing their chances of freedom. This led to an increase in the number of free people of color, creating a third tier of society, made up of skilled workers and militiamen. However, this freedom was never guaranteed and remained vulnerable to revocation, with many free people of color losing their autonomy during the colonial and antebellum periods. Despite this, free people of color in New Orleans developed into a cohesive group that gained a sense of agency.

Much of the Spanish leadership married into Creole families and did little to change the French social customs in the colony. For instance, Governor Bernardo de Gálvez gladly embraced French Creole traditions, and as a result, the number of celebrations increased. Through his familial connections with Creole families, he promoted trade with France and expanded Gallic influence in the city. Public masked balls continued to be popular in Spanish colonial New Orleans.[24]

In 1781, the city council debated whether Black and white individuals should refrain from gathering to celebrate Carnival while the Spanish were fighting the British on the Gulf Coast. Spanish soldiers and crew members of these ships, many of whom were Black, both free and enslaved, allegedly broke into groups to roam around and search for balls to attend. According to Spanish authorities, these visitors took advantage of the local Carnival tradition of masking to patronize the dance halls and attend dances in private homes. Consequently, it was decided to prohibit all people of color from masking and nighttime dancing, using the war as a pretext to restrict and segregate them while ignoring the established rights of those who were free; additional ordinances would follow.[25] Thus, the mixing of enslaved and free people of color with the white population at public masked balls was already a concern for the city council in New Orleans by 1781, indicating that the first public dance venue had likely been constructed by then.[26]

Even Indigenous Americans were seen dancing the night away, adorned in little more than traditional loincloths.[27] In 1787, one such ball entertained thirty-six Choctaw and Chickasaw Indian chiefs invited by Governor Miró.[28] Given that dancing was a significant feature of both the social and religious lives of the Indigenous inhabitants, this should not have been surprising. Historically, missionaries in New France who did not frown on or prohibit activities such as dancing had more positive relationships with Indigenous people, mirroring earlier dealings between them and the coureurs du bois. Marc Bergier, a missionary who worked with the Tamarois tribe, failed miserably in his interactions with them because he disapproved of their cultural differences, including their dances *impudiques,* or indecent dances, particularly on Good Friday. When he died, they danced in thankfulness for his passing.

In 1786, amid rising concerns about the growing class of free people of color in Louisiana, Miró enacted the *Bando de buen gobierno* (Edict for Good Government). This law mandated that all Black women cover their heads with tignons—headscarves or turban headdresses—and prohibited them from wearing silks, feathers, or jewels, thereby blurring the distinction between the free and the enslaved.[29]

Meanwhile, in Paris, public masked balls were held as early as 1715, but by 1789, the streets were filled with more unruly masked citizens than usual.[30] This public disorder soon led to the absolute banning of masks and masked balls because French revolutionaries viewed masking not as an expression of freedom but as "the opposite of liberty," arguing that masks "expressed the servitude of life under a tyranny." After the Revolution, masks had no place in Parisian life except for the aristocracy and only for one reason: to prevent them from being identified by the prying eyes of the citizens. Aristocrats donned disguises as peasants to escape the city, avoid capture, flee the country, and perhaps avoid the guillotine. Numerous tales emerged of bedraggled women trudging through towns dressed in rags, concealing their soft hands and skin. Even more troubling, aristocrats put on disguises as they gathered and conspired as counterrevolutionaries.

By 1790, Carnival in Paris had been rebranded as an unmasked patriotic celebration with two public dances called "bals non masqué." City ordinances banned masking and forbade stores from selling or displaying costumes or masks. Those brave enough to disobey orders were threatened with imprisonment and fines for all their masked guests. However, after Robespierre's execution, masking returned to Paris, even though the ban would not be officially lifted until 1805, at Napoleon's order.[31]

Across the Atlantic Ocean, far from the French Revolution yet still influenced by it, masking in New Orleans became controversial once again, not because of fear of aristocratic escapes but of fear of enslaved people, whose ears caught whispers of revolutions of those in physical bondage. Dances were legal for white colonists unless specified otherwise, but the relaxed rules surrounding racial segregation in New Orleans remained a point of contention for years to come. The ballroom, often a site of controversy and an accessible venue for resistance for people of color, faced periodic criticism. Masked balls were particularly problematic because a mask could hide one's race or even conceal one's enslavement, leading to a potential mixing of races that could erupt in uprisings. One legitimate fear was that liberal whites would influence enslaved people to seek freedom. George Washington Cable begins his book *The Grandissimes,* set in 1804 at a masquerade ball, "to play up the theme of masking and concealment around the issues of true identity," suggesting that many in Louisiana were of mixed descent but were hiding their true identities, raising fears that mixed-race individuals might have sympathies for their enslaved kin.[32]

Bernard Coquet, a recent immigrant from Saint-Domingue, played a pivotal role in transforming entertainment in New Orleans.[33] He hosted balls at his residence, but after acquiring the lease for the ballroom on Condé Street, he organized separate nighttime dances for white adults, for free people of color, and for children.[34] These balls quickly gained popularity, with more than five hundred people at times packed into halls to dance to music performed by "people of colour" or gypsy fiddlers.[35] Admission was affordable, with tickets costing fifty cents for men, while women were admitted free of charge.

By the end of the eighteenth century, three types of balls emerged in New Orleans: private balls given by the upper class for family, business associates, and friends; "society balls" organized by upper- and middle-class patrons, which included subscription balls where tickets were sold in advance, usually at the beginning of the season and often in a series costing as much as ten dollars; and "public balls" that had to be licensed by the city and were open to the public with the purchase of a ticket.[36]

New Orleans was a small town experiencing rapid growth. The residents, tired of intimate gatherings, clamored for an official public ballroom; perhaps the influx of "foreign French" following the French Revolution and those fleeing the impending revolution in Saint-Domingue, which began in 1791, contributed to this demand. Eventually, the Cabildo, the Spanish administrative governing council, recognized that these balls could generate revenue for the perpetually cash-strapped colony. Filiberto Farge requested that a new hall be built on the site of the King's Warehouse at the intersection of Dumaine and Condé Streets, which would be named the Condé Street Ballroom, or La Salle Condé.[37] It opened on the very same night—October 4, 1792—as the first private theater in New Orleans, which was built by two brothers from Paris. Jean-Marie Henry had been living in New Orleans where he was working as a *perruquier,* or wigmaker, when his brother Louis arrived in 1788—possibly to help rebuild the city after a fire earlier that year. They built the theater on a small lot now recognized as 732 St. Peter Street. By 1793, it was already known as a "lowlife ballroom" filled with "cutthroats" and was referred to as the notorious "*spectacle de la rue Saint Pierre.*" The ballroom received much more positive reviews. The Baroness de Pontalba noted in a letter to former Spanish Governor Miró that it was "quite beautiful and spacious."[38]

On November 1, 1792, just one month after La Salle Condé opened, the new Spanish governor, Francisco Luis Hector Carondelet, enacted new ordinances to regulate the behavior of people of color in New Orleans.[39] Fears that unrest from nearby Saint-Domingue would infiltrate New Orleans reinforced his intention to prohibit both free and enslaved people of color from wearing masks.[40] By wearing masks, enslaved individuals could socialize more easily with free people at balls, both Black and white. Cécile Vidal explained that the "space that slaves created through their nighttime sociability was neither public nor private but secret," creating a realm for various intrigues. In New Orleans, masked balls became venues where race was defined yet, despite the laws, identities could also be concealed there.[41]

In 1795, the third Thursday of Lent, or mid-Lent, fell on March 19. Curiously, a letter from Spanish civil servant Don Andrés Almonaster y Roxas de Estrada to Bishop Peñalver of New Orleans suggested that the "*feria,*" or festival, should be held on Sundays during Lent at the cathedral.[42] In what is now Mexico, *ferias* were celebrated in the 1700s. They generally began as a day of religious observance that segued into secular activities, such as bullfighting and an open market traditionally set up outside the church.[43] The civil servant's suggestion may have been an effort to tone down masking and dancing on mid-Lent in New Orleans by offering an alternative celebration at the cathedral, sanctioned by the church and overseen by non-French leadership. Kimberly S. Hanger suggests that these "church-sponsored attempts to direct moral behavior and enticed parishioners into the church and away from 'depraved' forms of recreation."[44] No further mention of these *ferias* exists, and the popularity of masked balls endured.

In 1799, an Irishman from Connecticut visited New Orleans. He was surprised to find "over one hundred [N]egroes of both sexes assembled on the levee, fiddling, dancing, and singing" on February 24 and again on March 3, the third and fourth Sundays of Lent that year.[45] Kinser notes that during the colonial period "the fourth Sunday in Lent was the occasion of a revival of Carnival in many European locales" and that "New Orleans's custom of St. Joseph's Day became the equivalent of European Mid-Lent," which 'became rather a substitute for Ash Wednesday as the terminal date for the enjoyment of dancing." He also explains that St. Joseph's Day was a "momentary resumption of Carnival games," possibly a reference to masking, which was still prohibited.[46]

Meanwhile, appealing to the cash-strapped city, Coquet and his business partner José Boniquet agreed to underwrite the expenses of a local playhouse, El Coliseo, in exchange for the exclusive rights to host balls there for free people of color.[47] In April 1799, the Cabildo authorized Coquet to hold "colored balls." However, in February 1800, Attorney General Pedro Barran urged the council to reduce the number of public dance halls, explicitly referring to Coquet and claiming that enslaved people were often seen attending events at his other venue, the theater on St. Peter Street. Barran also claimed that Coquet's balls had become "a ridiculous imitation of Farge's dances," where free people of color "imitate the luxury of the whites."[48] In turn, Coquet asserted that all the enslaved attendees had written permission from their owners, in accordance with the prevailing law; however, many believed these rules were rarely followed and that "most of the slaves in the city frequented this ballroom."[49] The Cabildo then ruled that "colored dances" could only take place in private homes, with no "whites" permitted at all.[50]

Free people of color continued to build their community life, however, with the most prominent social activities being dances and balls. They demanded the right to hold and attend these events. On October 24, 1800, four members of the free Black militia presented a letter to the Cabildo, expressing concern that their authorization to hold balls might be revoked on their return from a recent military campaign. The men requested permission from the Cabildo's leadership to hold balls on Saturdays during Carnival. Hence, the "dance will not interfere with the one the white people regularly have, for they have their dance on Sundays." They revealed that through "the kindness of Don Bernardo Coquet, we have his permission to use his house for dances. We ask that you be kind enough to the petitioners to provide them with the guards of the city who previously guarded the house when dances were given to prevent disorders."[51] These "disorders" were caused by "mainly white hooligans," which indicated that whites at this time were still attending balls for people of color.

In 1801, a similar problem arose when it was reported that "seamen, soldiers, and country folk—that is, whites–were resorting to the free black ballroom!"[52] Balls could both create and erase racial lines, and many members of the white Creole elite disapproved of any form of mixing. Yet New Orleanians who were not members of the elite "refused to conform to any solidified social stratification based on race, class, or legal status." Despite being officially segregated, many New Orleanians of different races mingled at private balls, such as those held at the home of the wealthy free Black man, Esteban Lalande.[53]

As the population of free people of color grew, so did the demand for social activities. Balls specifically tailored to free people of color nurtured the development of their own identity, distinct from that of both white individuals and enslaved people. These events created a space where group identity flourished, taking full shape during the antebellum period when the pervasive biracial caste system began to solidify. However, by employing guards at their balls and excluding specific individuals, free people of color established a third tier of society: a space for themselves that was neither white nor enslaved.[54] They distinguished themselves not only from enslaved people but also from lower-class white residents, acknowledging that as "free blacks" they were citizens, yet of a different class.[55]

During his "reign of twenty days," French Prefect Pierre Clément de Laussat, who engineered the colony's transition from Napoleon's France to Jefferson's United States, observed that "social and cultural life is as developed here as it is in Paris" and that another former French colony, Saint-Domingue, was a significant contributor to life in New Orleans. He said, "I imagine that Saint-Domingue was, of all our colonies in the Antilles, the one whose mentality and customs influenced Louisiana the most. Frequent intercourse existed between the two. Even today when the Negroes, having become independent, have chased us from Haiti, exiles from the island prefer Louisiana as a refuge. One meets many former settlers from there who are given shelter in Louisiana by relatives and friends."[56]

Those fleeing Saint-Domingue first brought their French customs to the very Spanish colony of Cuba, but many left there for New Orleans. In his fictionalized account of the Haitian Revolution, author Alejo Carpentier elaborates that on their first stop, "passepieds and contredanses were heard for the first time in Santiago de Cuba. The latest wigs, worn by the daughters of the French settlers, twirled to the rhythm of lively minuets already forecasting the waltz. The winds of license, of fantasy, of disorder, blew through the city."[57] Even as refugees, luxury items and dancing were deemed to be necessities.

In 1802, Berquin-Duvallon, a planter from Saint-Domingue who had fled the Haitian Revolution and stayed for a time in Baltimore, visited a public ball in New Orleans, likely at La Salle Condé. He noted that the hall was merely a colossal barrack in an "unfortunate part of the city, that is only accessible through mud and mire" and that the place was "miserably lighted; no chandeliers, but simple candles." He revealed that the musicians playing at the ball were "half a dozen gypsies or else people of color, scraping their fiddles with all their might" and pointed out that, except for the band, the crowd was white: they danced *grosso modo,* a rowdy style of country dancing. He noted that New Orleans was backward yet metropolitan, despite having only about ten thousand inhabitants in the city and its suburbs. He said, "It is too a tessellated pavement; here a Creole, there an Englishman; here a Frenchman, there a Spaniard; here a German, there an Italian. It is a tower of Babel; various are the dialects."[58] A later description of balls in New Orleans as "unique affairs" painted a picture of the ballroom as a "long, dingy, framed building."[59] Surprisingly, these balls usually lasted until morning.[60]

Napoleon devastated the entire Creole community when he sold Louisiana to the United States. Even though the French had not ruled Louisiana for generations, it "never became Spanish in a cultural sense, and it would be a French city when the United States took over in 1803."[61] Laussat proclaimed that, despite the years of Spanish rule, "Louisianians are Frenchmen at heart!"[62]

Yet Laussat noted that the Americans were already in New Orleans, exerting their influence by the time he arrived in the city. On April 18, 1803, he observed that the "Anglo-American flag eclipses by its number here those of France and Spain. In front of the city and along its quays, there are at this moment fifty-five Anglo-American ships to ten French. They are poisoning these countries with English goods, with which the French goods cannot compete," as the English goods had no duty taxes.[63]

Yet many of the troubles that the Americans faced as New Orleans made the transition from a European colony to an American state began in the ballrooms. James Pitot, a Frenchman born in Normandy and educated in Paris, who had lived in Philadelphia before arriving in Spanish-held New Orleans in 1796, was appointed mayor by Governor Claiborne in 1804. Often referred to as the first American mayor because of his US citizenship, he decidedly did not approve of many of the balls in the city: he declared that public balls were "where those who have a bit of discretion prefer not to appear, organized by free people of color. . . . [It] is each week the gathering place of the scum of such people and of those slaves who, eluding their owner's surveillance, go there to bring their plunder" and that "as a crowning infamy one finds even some white people who repeatedly battle with the slaves for places in the quadrilles." Pitot concluded, "Louisianians were always Spanish in name, French at heart, and often ran the risk of contraband trade with foreigners."[64]

C. C. Robin, a French botanist who documented his travels through Louisiana, acknowledged the roughness of the area at the time: "Louisianians are strangers alike to art and science or even the most ordinary items of knowledge. Therefore, they play, and play heavily." He elaborated on this idea when explaining his views on balls in New Orleans: "Winter is the season of balls and they are very frequent. There are public balls, both for ladies of quality, which means whites and for the colored women. The men go to both. The stiffness and aridity of the great ladies make these balls extremely dull for those who do not gamble. The others show much more vivacity but not the kind everyone likes."

Robin was also upset by the treatment of women of color at the balls.

He reported an incident in which two "quadroon" women attending a ball were called out for being of "mixed blood" and forced to leave. He pointed out that the two women were well educated and that the "blamelessness of their conduct" was known, but they were still treated poorly.[65] This vignette raises the intriguing notion of "passing" and whether other women at this or other balls were perceived as "white" but were not.

3

ANTEBELLUM ST. JOSEPH'S DAY

Statehood and the Emergence of Creole Culture

What other American city is so strongly flavored with Mediterranean Catholicism, with Carnivals that bridge the chasm between the sacred and profane with such élan?

—PEIRCE F. LEWIS, *New Orleans: The Making of an Urban Landscape*

Part of the myth and the truth of New Orleans is that it has long been a crossroads of different cultures, often in conflict, sometimes in harmony.

—CHRISTOPHER BENFEY, *Degas in New Orleans*

On December 20, 1803, the flag of the United States was raised at the Place d'Armes. Soon after, the first signs of discontent and cultural clashes between the Creoles and Americans became evident at prominent public balls. Governor William C. C. Claiborne quickly realized that the transition would face some challenges because he was an administrator of a "quasi-colonial territory inhabited by a culturally foreign population."[1] Indeed, Claiborne was attempting to conquer a somewhat strange land.

Tensions ran high from the earliest rumors of the Louisiana Purchase. The Spanish were outraged, seeing the sale as entirely illegitimate, and the residents of New Orleans feared a full-scale invasion by the Anglo-

Americans. The Francophile New Orleanians were concerned about the perceived threat to their cultural identities and practices, including dancing and balls—two passions many inhabitants cherished as direct links to their French heritage. Cultural life in Creole New Orleans was also and continues to be closely tied to Catholic celebrations, which sharply contrasted with colonial American ideals.

Less than two weeks after the American flag was raised, Claiborne noted with concern in a letter to Secretary of State James Madison that the "Season of Festivity" was upon them and that "frivolous diversions seem to be among their primary pleasures."[2] Soon after, on January 8, trouble broke out at a public ball over the local line dances because "two quadrilles, one French, the other English, formed at the same time. An American, taking offense at something, raised his walking stick at one of the fiddlers. Bedlam ensued." The melee continued until someone yelled, "If the women have a drop of French blood in their veins, they will not dance." With this comment, the women stopped dancing and abandoned the hall. Claiborne then realized two things: that the people of New Orleans were deeply attached to all things French and that balls were more than just a minor distraction. He was determined to ensure that the people of New Orleans "do not clash over things more serious and important," but trouble at the balls persisted.[3]

In another letter to Madison written on January 10, Claiborne confessed that a "*fracas*" at a public ball was "worthy of mentioning." He noted that the dispute started over which type of dance would have precedence: "the American or French Dances."[4] Americanness had not yet solidified, so much of what the Americans brought to New Orleans was perceived as English because of their shared heritage. At the time, the French were sworn enemies of the English. In addition to the problematic sale of the territory to the Americans, the English-style dances seemed like another threat to New Orleanians' Frenchness because American dances were often based on English ones.

Balls continued to be sites of conflict, and on January 22, Claiborne and James Wilkinson, the first governor of the Louisiana territory, relayed an account of yet another incident to James Madison. This time, "French officers and troublesome young Men from Bordeaux were the Aggressors," demanding that no *Contra Danse Anglaise* be performed because of its connection to the English.[5] These Frenchmen likely had arrived in New Orleans via Baltimore and Philadelphia, fleeing the revolution in France, or perhaps they were passing through the city on ships from Bordeaux and Nantes after the latest failed French attempt to quell the troubles in Saint-Domingue.[6]

Unrest was again feared on January 24 when a "ball began in a generally bad atmosphere. The city officials decided that one should dance successively two rounds of French quadrilles, one round of English quadrilles in groups of twelve partners, and one round of waltzes." However, conditions quickly deteriorated, causing most women to flee the scene. Two Frenchmen were cited in court but were later released.[7]

In response to these incidents, the new government in late January established the "Police of the Ball," assigning a militia officer and fifteen men to each event. Claiborne concluded that "this Gallant duty" be "cheerfully surrendered to the Municipality of the City," rejecting his title as Regulator of the Balls that previous governors had gladly accepted and thereby raising more suspicions about Americans within Creole society.[8] Additional regulations were introduced to ease tensions and control tempers at the balls, including requirements that weapons be checked at the door and that no song could be stopped once started.[9]

Yet, on January 31, Claiborne found it necessary to report to Madison that some French officers and citizens "seem to foster great hatred to the Americans who are here," that the Public Ballroom has been the "Theatre of all this Disorder," and that the people of New Orleans were firm in their defense of this one tradition. The amount of time spent discussing these balls is astounding, considering all that needed to be accomplished at that time to transfer power and establish a new government.

Most Anglo-Americans did not comprehend the significance of this pastime, but the popularity of these balls made them impossible to ban completely. In addition to dancing itself, fraternization between races at the balls became a source of contention for Americans, especially because such interactions and integration were rare in other parts of the United States.[10] These misunderstandings often resulted in "bloody duels between the Creoles and *les Américains.*"[11]

The instigators in each incident varied depending on who told the story about it, their backgrounds, and personal sympathies. Many blamed visiting Frenchmen for igniting this dance controversy. Regardless of who instigated the conflicts, they revealed fundamental cultural differences and tangible resentment on both sides.

Unfortunately, disturbances at the balls continued, and on February 10, a letter from Creole planter and the first mayor of New Orleans, Etienne de Boré, to President Jefferson reported more troubles surfacing between the Creole inhabitants of New Orleans and the newcomers, *les Américains.* Once again, these spaces proved to be battlegrounds for resistance to American rule:

> I have observed, with infinite pain, that disputes have come to light in recent days. It is unfortunate to begin like this. We would not expect to see this spirit of discord and division emerging among pleasures and dances, amid a large circle of women who make up their charm and beauty. You need to know the truth. The disputes have been fostered and even fomented by those whose responsibility it is to control them. The hotheadedness of people who are greedy for influence at any price contributes to large measure. These people are responsible for misleading those in power and having them undertake inappropriate measures.
>
> I am taking the risk of telling you this, Mister President. It is essential that the leaders of Louisiana speak French as well as English. If they had had that advantage, we would not have witnessed the events that produced such a bad impression; things would not be languishing, and we would not be in such difficulty.[12]

Claiborne recognized that the French language needed to be preserved, at least for the time being. He also decided that dancing was as important as the language for the city's Creoles. Even though many of his fellow Americans considered dancing and balls trivial and thought that dance halls were "morally questionable,"[13] Claiborne promised to allow balls to continue, alleviating some of the Creoles' anxieties.[14]

Initially, the Louisiana Purchase did little to reduce France's influence on the newly minted US territory, partly because of Napoleon Bonaparte's treaty stipulation that allowed Frenchmen to trade under the same terms as citizens of the United States for twelve years.[15] Many New Orleanians retained their connections to Paris for various non-economic reasons as well—to buy ball gowns and costumes and to engage in other aspects of French culture. Claiborne also worried about several hundred immigrants from Jamaica, who likely came to New Orleans after migrating from Saint-Domingue.[16] Eventually, Anglo residents began to weave themselves into the city's social fabric. However, as Americanization materialized, a potent form of Creole identity emerged, creating a space for cultural exchange. "Creole became an idea to shape Louisiana's past, a conception indicating social and cultural exceptionality in the present, and a birthright conferring dominion over New Orleans's future."[17]

Balls continued to be held but had to follow new regulations, including using designated dance setlists, as the new Americans attempted to negotiate and understand, both figuratively and literally, the French-leaning residents of New Orleans. After arriving in town in the mid-1800s, Frederick Law Olmsted soon noticed "French noises and French smells," as well as "French signs, ten to one of English"; even the English speakers' language was peppered with French. He was amused by the Irish driver's response to a question: "*Oui,* yer 'onor."[18]

Negotiating race posed another dilemma for the new Americans. "For Anglo-Americans, it was difficult to imagine a social context within which it would be acceptable for a white person to associate so liberally with a person of color on terms that would even remotely suggest equality."[19] Americans' more rigid attitudes toward race would permeate all facets of life after the failure of Reconstruction.

Under French and Spanish rule, racial mixing was not necessarily favored, but it was accepted within Creole society. New Orleans was never a segregated city, challenging the American approach to race relations that was rooted in British systems in which physical separation was crucial. In most of the United States, Black inhabitants were confined to specific areas, in contrast to the proximity of races in New Orleans.[20] During Louisiana's colonial period, many people of color were highly skilled, establishing their own institutions and venues reflecting an elevated social status, suggesting that the "highly racialized society thus failed to produce an explicitly racialized landscape."[21]

In 1806, a new Black Code was instituted with the assistance of the white Creole elites, who remained in power but worried about their status after the Louisiana Purchase.[22] This new code mirrored the more rigid racial system already present in the rest of the United States and much of the French Caribbean, including Saint-Domingue, whose refugees would help shape the social life of the city.[23]

New Orleans's racial ideas continued to challenge the new Americans. In 1808, the Louisiana Civil Code included a new law prohibiting mixed-race New Orleanians from marrying Blacks and whites. Not surprisingly, the Catholic Church continued to perform clandestine weddings in direct defiance of the law, and many couples opted to live openly as unmarried people with children and families.[24] Catholic New Orleanians confused the Anglo-Americans in various ways.

Given the troubles at the balls, the New Orleans City Council prohibited masking in public spaces, including the streets and ballrooms, and outlawed masked balls altogether.[25] Reportedly, no masked balls were held between 1804 and 1805. An ordinance passed on January 21, 1806, extended the masking ban for at least another year, imposing fines of ten dollars for hosting and twenty dollars for attending public or private masked balls in New Orleans. The mayor urged the City Council to lift the ban, but it refused to do so.[26]

Over the years, many ballroom owners and managers requested permission to hold masked balls but to no avail. The City Council consistently denied such requests because the early years of American rule were permeated by fear and anxiety generated not only by local incidents of violence at balls but also by the nearby Haitian Revolution, the Slave Revolt of 1811, and the War of 1812.[27] The prospect of enslaved people mingling at masked balls with each other or even with liberal-thinking whites or free people of color heightened fears of local rebellion.

Joseph Bonaparte, Napoleon's brother, played a crucial role in a subsequent wave of French influence on the city, undermining the aspirations of an American Republic founded on Protestant values. After fleeing the Haitian Revolution, immigrants from Saint-Domingue were sent to Cuba. Napoleon had his sights set on the island for his brother's rule, and when this news reached the Spanish government in Cuba, the Saint-Domingue refugees were forced to either marry a Spaniard or pledge allegiance to the king of Spain or risk deportation.[28]

In Cuba, a "riot against the French immigrants" on March 21, 1809, prompted many to flee to nearby New Orleans: these lively Catholic French-speaking whites, free people of color, and enslaved people nearly doubled the city's French-speaking population.[29] Their influx revitalized French Catholic ideals in the newly acquired territory.[30] "The Louisiana Purchase did not sever the connections between New Orleans and the Antilles. Quite the opposite happened."[31] Those French Creoles already living in New Orleans suddenly found allies who shared their love for "frivolous" masked balls and a tripartite understanding of race, ideas that were utterly foreign to the new Anglo-Americans, who viewed race in binary terms of Black and white. Americans' anxiety over racial mixing later led to changes in celebrating holidays like St. Joseph's Day.

Saint-Domingue, the most profitable French colony in the West Indies, boasted nearly 800 sugar plantations on which toiled a half-million people.[32] The tiny island produced more sugar than any other island, and this wealth led to the development of an advanced society. In 1717, one administrator from Saint-Domingue reported that no one wanted to do business with Louisiana because it had so few inhabitants and even fewer commodities.[33] Years later, François Barbé-Marbois, France's financial minister at the time of the Louisiana Purchase, observed that "Louisiana has been enriched by the disasters of Saint Domingo, and the industry that gave so much value to that island now fertilizes the Valley of the Mississippi."[34] The immigrants introduced agricultural innovations and infused their unique Creole French culture into existing traditions. Their migration "eventually reinforced Louisiana's cultural exception in the United States as well as Louisiana's conscious efforts to dissent from the rest of the American South" and brought a much more advanced social life to New Orleans, "which left room for the immigrants to exert an influence in many sectors."[35]

Of this influx, Nathalie Dessens notes, "Little has been written in this, except that the arrival of the [Saint-Domingue] refugees coincided with the expansion of the masked balls and Carnival processions, which until then had been forbidden by the Cabildo." Under Spanish rule, "people of color were forbidden to wear masks and attend night balls. Although the first reference to masking during Carnival in Louisiana dates to 1781, the practice gained momentum when the refugees reached Louisiana, perhaps as a pushback against the Anglo-Americans."[36] The Saint-Domingue immigrants, by their sheer numbers, strengthened the French masking traditions that were probably already in place. The Americans continued to outlaw masked balls, but minutes of New Orleans City Council meetings and the passage of ordinances regulating them reveal that they could not be stopped altogether.

One of the earliest advertisements for a ball on St. Joseph's Day appeared on March 18, 1807, in the French-language newspaper *Le Moniteur de la Louisiane*. It announced *"a Grand Bal, Demain Jeudi, 19 du courant, Grand Bal Paré Dans la salle accoutumée, a l'occasion de la fête du jour."* The ad did not mention St. Joseph, but the ball likely took place then because it was New Orleans's mid-Lent; the following year, the same advertisement ran with the addition of *"Jour [Day] de la Saint-Joseph."*[37] Attempts to persuade the City Council to allow masking continued to fail, so no masked balls were given legally, but this does not mean that they were not to be found. Over the years, public demand for masking increased, and as the ads for masquerade balls on St. Joseph's Night showed, the laws were blatantly ignored.[38]

Edward Bertus, a recent émigré from Saint-Domingue and manager of the Condé Street Ballroom, likely sparked a revival of masked balls in New Orleans. In 1812, Bertus asked the City Council for permission to hold four masked balls. It declined, but he persisted; in 1814, he and Chéry, the new

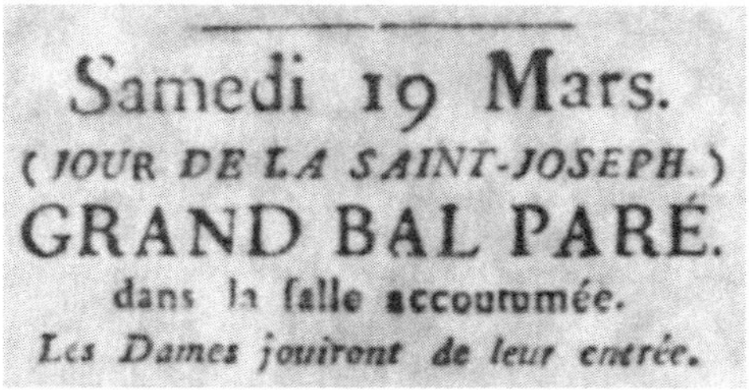
Samedi 19 Mars.

(JOUR DE LA SAINT-JOSEPH.)

GRAND BAL PARÉ.

dans la ſalle accoutumée.

Les Dames jouiront de leur entrée.

Early advertisement for a St. Joseph's Day ball in the French-language newspaper *Le Moniteur.* This one is dated March 16, 1808.

lessee of the Condé Street Ballroom and a dancing master, requested a permit to host three masked balls. Once again, the City Council refused, even though Bertus and Chéry offered to donate one-third of their profits to charity. In 1817, the Orleans Theatre and Ballroom opened amid great excitement. Located where the Hotel Bourbon Orleans is today, it was very different from the Condé Street Ballroom, which was described as a "big, wooden barracks." Instead, the Orleans Theatre and Ballroom was characterized as "an immense hall, hung with rich draperies" and illuminated by large chandeliers, giving it a sense of elegance and culture. Bertus allowed attendees at his balls to dress in the Orleans Theatre's actors' costumes and masks, thereby implying respectability and broadening their appeal. He hosted these events, often masked, especially during Carnival and St. Joseph's Night, under the guise of dance classes rather than masked balls. His events became so popular that they were allowed to continue.[39] In 1823, Carnival records mention masked balls being held at the Orleans Theatre but offer few details.[40]

In 1824, a St. Joseph Day ball was advertised as unmasked: the ad specifically stated that anyone wearing a mask would not be admitted, which implied that people were still masking on the holiday, as confirmed by another newspaper.[41] Meanwhile, two ads found in the *Louisiana State Gazette* that same year show some balls were masked, two required subscriptions (tickets to attend more than one ball at the hall had to be purchased in advance), and the third advertised "a Grand Exhibition of Gas: To be succeeded by a splendid Masquerade Ball," promising the room would be "brilliantly illuminated." Children were allowed in for half-price at this Saturday ball that would "commence at 3 o'clock. Masks may be obtained at Davis's Ball Room," likely referring to the Orleans Theatre and Ballroom, operated by Davis and Bertus at the time. It seems Bertus was involved with at least two of these events.[42] An ad for their "St. Joseph's Holiday" event at the Orleans Theatre and Ballroom describes extensive preparations for the ball. The ballroom and theater would be connected by a "floor raised above the pit," and the boxes "will be closed by panels painted by Mr. Fogliardi and representing a saloon." Security was also addressed: "Twenty commissaries will be named for the direction of the Ball and keeping good order." Finally, "all kinds of Masquerade Dresses may be had at a moderate hire, at the Theatre ward-robe."[43]

Women were usually admitted free when accompanying a gentleman, except for "Mardi Gras, George Washington's birthday, and St. Joseph's Day, when demand was high enough to enable proprietors to charge women too."[44] This practice confirms the importance of St. Joseph's Day in the social life of the people of New Orleans.

Timothy Flint visited New Orleans during Carnival in 1823 and discovered a city that felt strange to an outsider; the many irreligious activities held on Sundays were especially jarring. He said that New Orleanians "are the same gay, dancing, spectacle-loving race, that they are everywhere else. It is well known that the Catholic religion does not forbid amusements on the Sabbath. They fortify themselves in defending the custom of going to balls and the theatre on the Sabbath, by arguing that religion ought to inspire cheerfulness and that cheerfulness is associated with religion." To his surprise, many women attended Catholic mass on Sundays in their gowns and would go directly to balls after the service ended: they thus blended the sacred and the profane adding balls to the list of "every thing that can tempt avarice or the passions is here."[45]

In the early nineteenth century, immigration surged from places in addition to Saint-Domingue, transforming New Orleans into a truly cosmopolitan port town and one that became even more Catholic. A steady stream of people from France, Ireland, Germany, and the rest of the United States found their way to Louisiana, with many settling in the city. French culture faced challenges but contributed to "the first moments of the creation of a new culture, an era of both Americanization and Creolization."[46] These immigrants' arrival bolstered resistance to Americanization while simultaneously building the Creole culture that New Orleans is known for today. The city's social landscape changed forever, and New Orleans became a genuinely Creole city.

The so-called foreign French and other recent Catholic arrivals in the early nineteenth century certainly contributed to the celebration of St. Joseph's Day as mi-Carême, because masking and mid-Lent connections were familiar to most who had a Catholic upbringing. Until the 1820s, St. Joseph's Day celebrations were publicly accessible and open to anyone who could afford a ticket, because New Orleans had no private clubs then; however, they were segregated by law. During the early years of American rule, public street celebrations and parading seemed to gain in popularity.[47] Rather than ban traditional French and Spanish public masked balls, the Americans directed their efforts to "seizing control of the city and directing its destiny. Although they eventually succeeded, their takeover was neither easy nor ever complete."[48]

At the same time, Anglo-Americans themselves experienced a form of Creolization, and their attendance at balls, both masked and unmasked, suggested that their disapproval of such frivolity had diminished. Governor Claiborne attended numerous balls and became an active participant in the city's social life.[49] By engaging in local Creole society events, the governor became as much a New Orleanian as an American: the city transformed people.[50]

In the meantime, Americans refashioned these dancing holidays into their own "Northern American" concepts of society by holding more subscription balls or "society balls." They navigated the space between colonial Louisiana and American New Orleans at these gatherings. "Society balls" emerged as an alternative to the public balls open to everyone: they were neither public nor completely private and perhaps were a more "democratic" option. They were often sponsored by young men who sold subscriptions to a series of dances over the season, which allowed the men to bring female guests.[51] Meanwhile, public balls were popularly depicted as a lowbrow form of entertainment that often ended in brawls. Public masked balls were even more scandalous. St. Joseph's Day balls concluded the social season, making this holiday crucial in yet another way.

In 1827, the New Orleans City Council convened to discuss renewing the ban on masking for the year. When 200 men presented a signed petition advocating for the legalization of masking, it finally agreed to legalize masked balls, but only from January 1 until the beginning of Lent.[52] With this law, the Anglo-led City Council decreed that masking would be exclusively associated with Carnival, thereby excluding St. Joseph's Day that occurs during Lent. The ordinance was passed on December 31, 1827, masking returned to the city, and the people celebrated. The local French newspaper, *L'Abeille,* proclaimed, "At last disguises are going to reappear. By a decision of the City Council, the mayor is authorised to permit masquerades, from the 1st of January to Mardi Gras. Rejoice. . . . Masks are permitted!"[53]

A few days later, on January 4, 1828, the City Council passed a shocking new ordinance: white men were no longer permitted to attend balls, whether masked or unmasked, that were held for women or men of color.[54] Although this law was unlikely to stop the mingling of races at these balls, it represented another effort to control race mixing—an American obsession. Balls for people of color would continue while excluding whites, at least on paper, a deviation from the city's earliest traditions.

That same year, *L'Abeille* contained two advertisements—one in English and the other in French—for a St. Joseph's Day ball at the "corner of Bourbon and Orleans." These ads stated that the ball was a "full dress ball and with characters. The same as are given in the principal cities in France and North America." This "kind of amusement not being well known here, the following explanation is given of it; each person may take any kind of disguise, without being masked, and in the dress which is represented by the dress, and which must be supported by the individual so disguised."[55]

Full dress balls and grand fancy dress balls allowed individuals to "assume a character of any description, or any nationality you like, but you must expose your features."[56] Masking was illegal after Mardi Gras, so attendees at balls during the rest of the year wore costumes that did not hide their faces. Although this ad suggests that these rules were observed, later ordinances reveal that masking was probably still a concern. After the ban was lifted on masked balls during Carnival, they returned in a surprising new venue, the Jackson Ballroom, located on New Levee and Girod Streets in the American part of town where many newcomers settled. Balls and dancing thus became an essential part of the social fabric of the new American city. Nathalie Dessens states, "Balls were a New Orleans institution."[57]

The allure of balls remained strong for Creoles in New Orleans, both Black and white, and their enthusiasm for integrated balls continued but not without controversy. Most ballrooms legally catered to all facets of the citizenry, albeit on different nights of the week. However, many references indicate that racial mingling was commonplace, particularly at dances requiring masks and particularly between whites and free people of color, who were a crucial and influential part of New Orleans society: many were highly skilled builders and artisans and owned property.[58] Creoles of color, both men and women, were active and respected community members and often met freely in public spaces such as balls until the Americans arrived.

Throughout the 1820s, Edward Bertus continued to host balls on St. Joseph's Day, although an ad for the 1829 ball incorrectly stated that March 19 was the "eve of the *Fête de St. Joseph*. . . . Gentlemen who accompany Ladies will pay three dollars, and will on subscribing give the name of the Ladies they will accompany. Gentlemen who do not accompany Ladies will pay 2 dollars—Gentlemen who will not have subscribed at the time of the opening of the Ball will pay three dollars. All tickets will be personal. E. BERTUS."[59] Masking was not mentioned, but Bertus was known to allow it because the balls were private affairs.

However, in 1830, despite the ban on masked balls after the Carnival season, an advertisement in *L'Abeille* promoted a grand dress and masked ball to be held at the Orleans Ballroom on St. Joseph's Day. Female guests likely received their tickets "during the Carneval, that, there will take place in the above BallRoom on March 19th, being St. Joseph"—linking the masked

Salle d'Orléans.

Bal de la St. Joseph.

L'ADMINISTRATION des bals de la Salle d'Orléans a l'honneur d'informer les Dames qui ont reçu dans le courant du Carnaval des billets d'invitation, qu'il y aura dans la dite salle, le jour de St. Joseph, 19 Mars, un

GRAND BAL

Paré et Masqué.

On n'y admettra que les dames qui recevront leurs billets d'invitation; elles sont priées de ne pas les oublier afin d'éviter l'inconvénian d'être retenues a leur entrée au bal.

Aucuu billet de dames ne sera délivré à la porte; celles qui u'en auront point ne seront point admises.

Les cavaliers payeront $1 50, en souscrivant sur le livre de souscription. 10 mars

An 1830 advertisement for a St. Joseph's Day ball in New Orleans.
L'Abeille, March 17, 1830.

balls on the two dates.[60] Perhaps the blatant disregard for its rules and regulations led the City Council to extend the masking season, as an ordinance approved on March 12, 1831, permitted masked or dress balls on St. Joseph's Day. This law designated St. Joseph's Day as the only official masking holiday outside the Carnival season, allowing residents to enjoy another carnival-like day with dancing.

In 1832, New Orleans suffered a widespread cholera epidemic, resulting in the cancellation of many balls.[61] Nevertheless, Creole New Orleanians continued to attend St. Joseph's Day masked balls the following year.[62] By 1834, the epidemic had affected so many people that balls and public entertainment were cancelled because the city was in mourning.[63]

Timothy Flint, in his travelogue, remarked that the women of New Orleans were "excessively attached to balls and parties"; allegedly, the daughter of the Voodoo queen of New Orleans was no exception.[64] In 1827, Marie

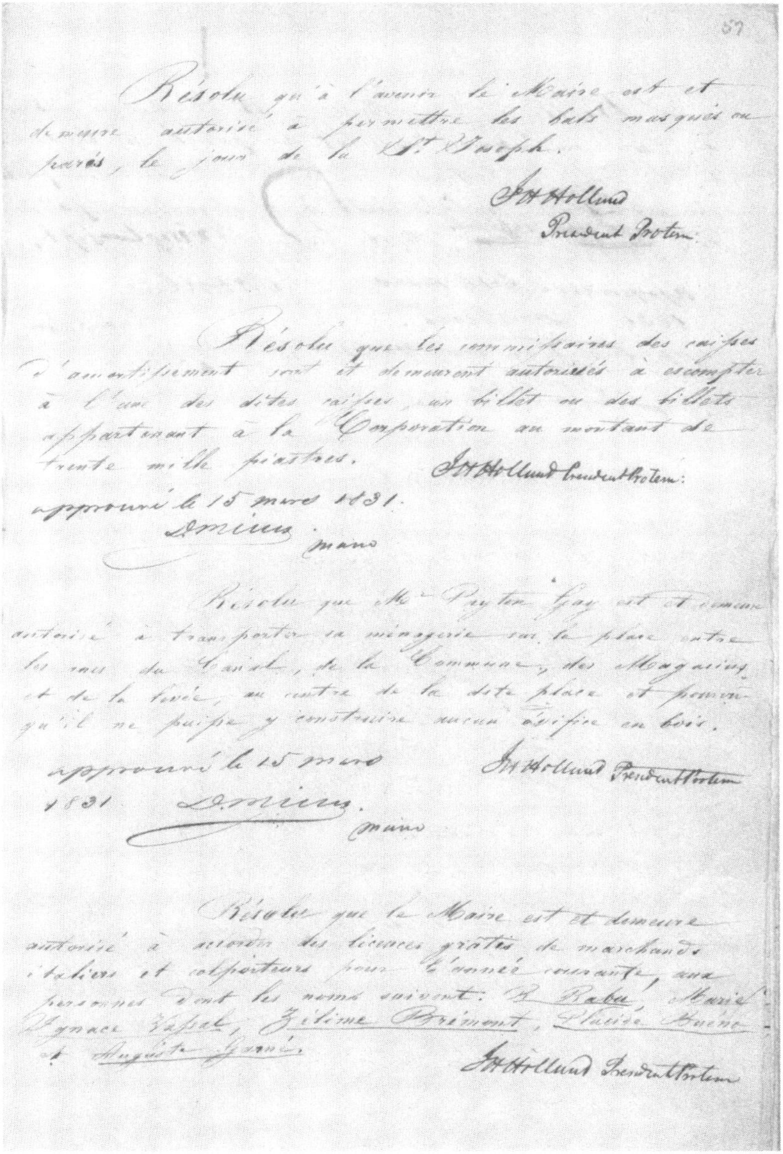
57

Résolu qu'à l'avenir le Maire est et demeure autorisé à permettre les bals masqués ou parés, le jour de la St. Joseph.

J.H. Holland
President Protem:

Résolu que les commissaires des caisses d'amortissement sont et demeurent autorisés à escompter à l'une des dites caisses un billet ou des billets appartenant à la Corporation au montant de trente mille piastres.

J.H. Holland President Protem:

approuvé le 15 mars 1831.
D. Prieur
maire

Résolu que Mr Peyton Gay est et demeure autorisé à transporter sa ménagerie sur la place entre les rues du Canal, de la Commune, des Magasins, et de la levée, au centre de la dite place et pourvu qu'il ne puisse y construire aucun édifice en bois.

approuvé le 15 mars 1831 D. Prieur maire

J.H. Holland President Protem

Résolu que le Maire est et demeure autorisé à accorder des licences gratis de marchands italiens et colporteurs pour l'année courante, aux personnes dont les noms suivent: B. Baba, Marie Ignace Vassal, Zilime Brimont, Placide Bueno et Augusta Garnier.

J.H. Holland President Protem

Ordinance (in French) allowing masking on St. Joseph's Night, March 15, 1831. New Orleans Public Library, Conseil de Ville, AB310, Ordinances and resolutions, 1805–1836. Subseries II, Vol. 16, page 57.

Laveau II was born of a *plaçage,* or domestic relationship, between her mother, free woman of color Marie Catherine Laveau, and the white man Christophe Dominick Duminy de Glapion. Luke Turner, who claimed to be Marie's nephew, was interviewed by novelist Zora Neale Hurston in the early 1900s about his "aunt." He revealed that Marie Laveau II almost forfeited her birthright because she was "very pretty, one of the Creole Quadroons and many people said she would never be a hoodoo doctor like her mama and her grandma before her. She liked to go to the balls very much where all the young men fell in love with her."[65]

John Latrobe also observed examples of racial mixing during his travels to New Orleans. In 1834 he saw "a most handsome barouche in which rode a white planter looking portly and well to do in the world, with his mulatto wife or mistress, a mulatto friend of hers and his mulatto children. Truly the state of society here is miserable enough: though I am informed that as the American resident population increases there is a change going on for the better."[66]

Even though this shocked him, he attended not one but two so-called Quadroon balls, which were supposedly open exclusively to white men and women of color: there, the men and women would be properly introduced, and many would then engage in long-term relationships. He described the dance on November 29 as the first ball of the season, which he was informed was "not fashionable" to attend, implying that the women in attendance were not the most desirable. He noted that there "were about forty women present of all shades, from the very dark mulatto to the light quadroon whose person bore no mark of her descent, and whose degradation and was a matter of tradition only. Nearly all had masks—white masks. Those who had not were young girls." No women wore costumes, although many men did and also wore masks. He soon realized that there were no white women in attendance.

Later that night he wandered down Royal Street, where he stumbled on another "Quadroon ball" at the Orleans Ballroom, which he felt was inferior to the St. Philip Street Ballroom because it had many "white women of the lowest order."[67] Concerns arose regarding "the composition of the masquerade balls" because "too many white women were attending masked balls intended for colored women," who brought with them "unprincipled men." City Council members noticed in 1835 that two-thirds of the women at one "*Quadroon* ball" were white, creating even more trouble and confusion.[68]

If "the French language in Louisiana served as a marker of distinction from, and a point of resistance against American rule," then celebrating a French Creole holiday like St. Joseph's Day acted as a badge of defiance against new Protestant settlers and their way of life.[69] Resistance to change began in New Orleans as early as 1762, when the French abandoned Louisiana; this led to a "mythological longing for connections to this lost homeland."[70] Rather than embracing American culture, in which citizens flaunted their Anglo-Saxon racial purity, New Orleanians remained proud of their ties to France through language, culture, and cuisine.[71]

In the early 1830s, a contemporary author noted that "every year the negroes have two or three holidays, which in New Orleans and the vicinity, are like the 'Saturnalia' of the slaves in ancient Rome." Samuel Kinser argues that two of these holidays were Christmas and Mardi Gras, but he does not give the identity of the third. One possibility is St. Joseph's Day, which was a day when costuming, disruption of social norms, and merrymaking were expected, much like the Roman holiday of Saturnalia.

In 1835, the mayor canceled the St. Joseph's Day ball at the Washington Ballroom due to rampant rumors that Americans were preparing for a brawl, "armed to the teeth," against the French and Creoles.[72] That very night, the American Ball Room promoted a Grand Full Dress and Masquerade Ball on the corner of Camp and Poydras Streets in the American part of town. And that very day, a very curious letter to the editor was published in the French-language newspaper *L'Advertiser:*

> Mr. Editor,
>
> It has been we believe, the established custom in this city, to devote St. Joseph's day, that half way house in the tedious desert of Lent, to festivities and amusements. St. Joseph's Day Ball, the last of the year, has always been looked upon by the laborious and industrious classes in our society as

> peculiarly their own fete,—and hundreds who could not afford to attend more than one ball have postponed their only holiday till St. Joseph's. It is now reported that the Mayor has ordered the Washington Ball Room, the most splendid in the United States, to be closed for the evening, from the apprehension (I need not say how unfounded that the American population of our city have formed a conspiracy to go to the ball to night, armed to the teeth for the purpose of committing a breach of the peace and driving the French and Creoles.
>
> We wish to express our regret that our excellent Mayor should have, for a moment, lent an ear to so unjust and unfounded an accusation. The American population, from whom so imminent a danger of a riot is apprehended, as to oblige the Mayor to close the Washington Ball Room, are generally the most peaceable class in society, and have long looked forward to this day as one of pleasure, not of riot and dissension. We take this means of expressing our wishes in hopes that the Mayor will revise his prohibition and permit the usual amusements of this day to proceed; and if their (sic) should be any riot occasioned by us, on us let the edinm (maybe edmin?) rest.
>
> MANY AMERICANS,
> The friends of Peace.[73]

This letter promised that the "Americans" had no intention of disrupting the ball that evening and pointed out that many people who could not afford to go to other balls usually attended one on St. Joseph's Day. It also highlighted the division among Americans, French, and Creoles in New Orleans. The tensions leading up to the St. Joseph's Day incident also helped explain why the ethnically diverse city was separated into three municipalities in 1836: each would operate as an independent city under the authority of a single mayor.[74] The city was culturally fragmented but more along an uptown/downtown or American/Creole split.[75] This segregation was possibly reinforced in the early 1800s by Bernard de Marigny, an old-line Creole property owner and former president of the Louisiana State Senate, who sold off his land to create a suburb just downriver from the French Quarter.

Notoriously anti-American, he denied the newcomers any commercial presence in the downtown area, thereby reinforcing the divide between uptown Americans and downtown Creoles that persists to this day.[76] Residents of the Creole municipalities exhibited a laissez-faire attitude toward enforcing laws, especially in the ballrooms, and as a result, rowdy Americans began infiltrating their dances, particularly the masked ones.[77]

In response, the First Municipality, a Creole area that included the French Quarter, passed a law banning masked balls in favor of fancy dress balls. It was revoked before it could be enforced, providing insight into the dynamics of an expanding city and the impact of external factors on the tight-knit Creole society struggling to maintain its way of life.[78] This debate also revealed that interethnic socializing existed and that the city was not as segregated as once believed, being both disconnected and connected in many ways.

Until the 1840s, Creoles controlled Carnival and other holidays, enhancing the notion of New Orleans as an exotic, European-style city with a distinct French cultural emphasis.[79] The *Daily Picayune* maintained that in 1838, "principally Creoles of the first respectability" still celebrated Mardi Gras, but this was about to change.

Irish-born journalist Louis Fitzgerald Tasistro noted during his visit to New Orleans in 1841 that many Anglo-American citizens regarded these holidays, including St. Joseph's Day, as "signs of the Catholic, French-speaking Creoles' frivolous mentality and general incapability to run Louisiana in an efficient way."[80] January, February, and March were the months where "people do nothing but dance during this period of cool and generally clement weather": the leisure-loving plantation society participated in winter festivals from Christmas to Lent. Mardi Gras Day was important not only for its celebrations but also because it marked the last day before Lent, during which balls were prohibited.[81] However, according to the *Daily Picayune* in 1841, the social season concluded not on Mardi Gras Day but with the Closing of the Balls on St. Joseph's Day as mid-Lent.[82] And so the social season lasted for five months, beginning in November, when cooler weather arrived, and ending with St. Joseph's Day, emphasizing its importance as the culmination of the year's festivities. The festivities would begin with the Christmas holidays, New Year's Eve and Day, and Twelfth Night—although January 6 did not then mark the start of the Carnival season as it does today. The balls held on Mardi Gras and St. Joseph's Night differed from others because masking was tied to tradition and culture, rather than merely serving as a strategy to sell tickets.

The number of public ballrooms increased to mirror the city's expansion. In 1805, there were fifteen public ballrooms, which expanded to thirty by 1815 and ballooned to more than eighty by the 1840s. Prices ranged from "$1.50 a couple to the six-dollar charge for box seats at the Orleans Theater."[83]

On March 19, 1849, the *New Orleans Daily Crescent* announced the conclusion of a ten-ball series on St. Joseph's Night in an unusual advertisement in this conservative English-language newspaper. The newspaper once hired Walt Whitman as a writer, but he quit, possibly because of his opposition to the expansion of slavery. On April 22, 1850, this same newspaper published an article elaborating on the cynical view many Americans and some Creoles held about balls and dance halls in New Orleans.

"The Private Character of Candidates for Office"

> Mr. J. H. Caldwell built the Camp Street Theatre and the St. Charles Theatre converted the Camp Street Theatre into a "dance house." A dozen or twenty years ago he hired out the Camp st. Theatre for a public ball room! which the Crescent says was the resort of loose women! A most tremendous crime was this in Mr. Caldwell! He rented out a building that belonged to him for a ball room! yes, a ball room! and the balls there in held were sometimes frequented by loose women! and loose men!—Courier

This article was also published in *Le Courier,* one of the French-language newspapers, and reprinted in the *New Orleans Daily Crescent.*[84] It described balls in which white men were allowed in freely; however, strict rules on female participation were enforced, even for white women, and concern about who frequented these balls became as much a point of contention as racial concerns. This attitude of moral superiority led Anglo-Americans to take Carnival into their own hands, ultimately creating a "new" more organized and exclusive Carnival that contributed to the eventual decline of St. Joseph's Day. In a sense, Mardi Gras evolved into a holiday that unified the city through its celebrations.[85] Everyone took part, although not necessarily together.

Eliza Ripley reminisced about a masquerade "society" ball given at the United States Mint building in New Orleans some sixty years later. The event left a lasting impression because she had not heard of a ball being hosted there before or since. She asked her audience: "Who was at the fancy ball? Everybody who was anybody in the fifties." No date was provided, so the reason the ball was given remains a mystery. She said the two daughters of the Kennedy family who threw the ball were debutantes that winter. She gushed about the talents of one sister whose performance of the Bamboula brought praise from its composer, Louis Moreau Gottschalk. The families involved were American, but on closer examination, most had some connection to the old Creole society through marriage, and all participated in frivolous "French" social diversions and frequented downtown spots. Uptown American elite society was not immune to the established, deeply rooted French celebrations brought over during the early days of settlement. They wore costumes rented from the "French opera troupe, and their faces were 'made up' with rouge that could not be washed off." Additionally, the reference to a white Anglo-American woman playing a song also known as "Danse des Nègres" by a local composer with mixed-race brothers and sisters illustrates how racially intertwined the city was at this time and how shocking it might have been to the rest of the country.[86]

In the mid-1800s, Frederick Law Olmsted quoted William Darby, the geographer and surveyor of Louisiana, as saying that dancing "might be called the principal amusement of both sexes, in Louisiana. Beholding the airy sweep of a Creole dance, the length of time that an assembly will preserve in the sport, at any season of the year, cold or warm, indolence would be the last charge that candor could lodge against such a people."[87] During a second visit, Olmsted stated that the Creole women of Louisiana were "languid, and incredibly indolent unless there was a ball, or some other excitement to engage them."[88]

Initially, Americans attempted to control the free people of color in the city by excluding them from social events. One of the first private balls organized by the Cowbellians group was held on St. Joseph's Day in 1853 at Union Hall. This Anglo-American society had no Creoles in its ranks and is said to have hosted the first-ever organized Mardi Gras parade in Mobile, Alabama.[89] Although this masked ball was not explicitly labeled as private, the lack of information about where to buy tickets led to the assumption that an invitation was required to attend.[90]

In 1837, the City Council granted free people of color and enslaved individuals the right to "give balls on the Circus Square [also known as Congo Square] from twelve o'clock until sunset under surveillance of the police."[91] Congo Square played a significant role in the history of resistance of enslaved people to their plight. However, in 1855, the police shut down the Globe Ballroom, which had opened in Congo Square in 1851, because it hosted integrated balls.[92] Curiously, just a few years later, in 1858, an advertisement noted that the Anglo-run Washington and American Ball Room, formerly the Globe, hosted Quadroon Balls throughout March.[93]

In the 1850s, new restrictions eroded many rights that free people of color had enjoyed since Spanish rule.[94] By 1852, the three municipalities had been eliminated. This consolidation, by shifting much of municipal power to state authorities, further diminished the rights granted to free people of color, starting with an attack on the somewhat lenient manumission requirements. After the Civil War, many Afro-Creole leaders would recall 1852 as the year their rights started to decline, as Anglo-American New Orleanians found their footing in the city and sought to control both culture and race.

Around this time, the state government sought to "remove free Blacks from their livelihoods, from their social standing, and from Louisiana."[95] In 1857, the governor requested that the state legislature order the expulsion of all mixed-race people from state; such a law was never passed. However, the state legislature did prohibit free people of color from forming charitable, literary, scientific societies, or religious organizations. Going one step further, the Anglo-American majority on the New Orleans City Council passed Ordinance 3847 in 1858, which restricted gatherings of any type of people of color.[96] Any person of African descent was legally required to obtain the mayor's permission for any meeting.[97] Although bureaucratic restrictions were not new to racially diverse New Orleans, this law aimed to create a monolithic idea of race that had not yet existed in the city. In antebellum New Orleans, "the free Negro was neither bound nor free. He was required to be respectful in the company of whites and to obtain the mayor's permission when leaving the city, holding balls, or forming social and benevolent societies." According to John Blassingame, the free man of color was "a quasicitizen–he bore much of the responsibility of citizenship with few of its privileges."[98]

In 1855, the *Daily Picayune* reported on a St. Joseph's Day ball held at the St. Charles Hotel in the American section of town; the article featured detailed descriptions of various costumes, which most dancers wore, and the activities throughout the night. Costumes depicted not only Catholic and French characters but also many figures from English literature, theater, and opera: the "motley mob of maskers; kings, queens, princesses, princes, emperors, lords, ladies, soldiers, priests, nuns, cardinals, ockies [*sic*], punchinellos, troubadours, debardeurs, matelots, porters, dandies, fortune-tellers, flower girls, vivandiers, filles de regiment, bloomers, ballet dancers, goddesses, representations of the morning and the night; in short, it would be difficult to say what was not as what was represented there." It is unclear whether the attendees were all Anglo-Americans or included Creoles who had ventured into the American Sector for entertainment.[99] *L'Abeille* complained that the old, established theaters were "killed" by the new, lavish American-run St. Charles Theater, the venue of this ball.[100]

Despite the legalization of segregation in New Orleans,[101] the theaters and ballrooms "welcomed the best Creole society of New Orleans of both colors."[102] The venue owners recognized that affluent free people of color would attend their events and support the arts in the city. Meanwhile, new legislation continued to be proposed to enforce segregation. Eventually, many balls became private functions that were closed to the public, eliminating any possibility of racial mixing.

In 1856, a group of New Orleans Anglo-American residents founded Comus, the city's first Carnival club. This led to an uproar because not a single Creole name was listed among its nineteen founding members. An article in *L'Abeille* called the members of Comus "swine-eating Saxons," stating that this latest iteration of Carnival was "not French or Italian and it bore almost no resemblance to any European variety, but was the original conception of an Irish and Dutch Pennsylvania American, at least as far as its outer trappings were concerned."[103]

Comus introduced further changes to Carnival in New Orleans, including a parade that was not only organized but also officially "closed,' meaning that only members could participate. This parade culminated in an elaborate ball at the Gaiety Theatre, which featured "tableaux vivants" as part of the evening festivities.[104] And so, the upper-class, white Anglo-American elites of New Orleans had claimed Carnival[105] at the same time that St. Joseph's Day balls were considered events for the lower classes.[106] Class standing assumed greater importance, although race mixing was still of concern.

After 1857, masked balls slowly evolved as being primarily associated with Carnival in New Orleans. They no longer were open to the public and charged a fee; their attendees were no longer a blend of races and classes. This was in contrast to colonial times when balls were more inclusive, and masked balls occurred throughout the year.[107] St. Joseph's Day emerged as one of the few holidays in the city to maintain its legal masking tradition outside the Carnival season for nearly another hundred years.

New Orleans has a rich history of showcasing its celebrations to tourists and locals, and St. Joseph's Day was no exception. In 1857, many attendees of one of the large dances that night were visitors, and they did not respect the masking traditions. As the *Picayune* noted, "We could never understand how the hundred bidden to a fancy dress and mask ball, as could be so few who have the civility to comply with the terms of their invitation." Although St. Joseph's Day balls as mid-Lent events occurred before 1857, the

Daily Picayune explained, "The Mi-Careme Festivities—St. Joseph's feast coming very near mid-lent this year, was selected as the general gala day and night, by the gay and fashionable, who made up for their long abstinence from amusement by entering with great zest into the festivities of the holiday. There were several private and public reunions in the different parts of the city, and the sound of merry music was heard among us until very near the dawn of another day."[108]

The growth of private balls on St. Joseph's Day during the first forty years of American rule showed "a clear progression toward the elaboration of a new cultural continuum borrowing from both dominant cultures, in which the two main groups would often meet halfway, building, in the process, a new original culture."[109] This culture evolved into a "common civil religion," in which celebrations became a unifying force in the struggle to coexist.

Social events, like St. Joseph's Day balls, were hosted initially in French ballrooms but eventually made their way to American venues. Advertisements in numerous newspapers, printed in both French and English, clearly indicated that the two factions of the city interacted socially. New holidays gained popularity, such as balls celebrating George Washington's birthday (possibly favored because it also occurred during Lent), demonstrating that Americans were becoming more Creolized.[110] French customs transformed Americans rather than the other way around. Eliza Potter, a free woman of color and hairdresser who moved to France from Cincinnati, said she was shocked that on Sunday evening after church, there were balls much like in New Orleans:

> [this] startled me a little at first; but it is astonishing how naturally we fall into the tastes and customs of people with whom we are for the time associated. I was miserable at first about it, and very much conscience-stricken at this innovation upon my usual American habits; but finally, *I regret to say,* I became as French as the rest of them, and dancing on the Sabbath evening, after the day had been spent in strict observance of religious duty, no longer offended by my notions of propriety.[111]

Like Eliza Potter, Anglo-Americans in New Orleans were no longer offended by the French Creole tradition of balls on Sundays and other days. Balls, especially on holidays such as Mardi Gras and St. Joseph's Day, served as catalysts for the white elites' power grab by embodying the ideology of race and exclusion.[112] The city was changing socially along with a physical transformation, in which the "geography of Creole New Orleans, concentrated in the Vieux Carré in the early part of the antebellum period, shifted below and behind the old city by the end of the antebellum era."[113] Physical changes in Creole New Orleans's geography revealed what was to come.

In 1861, as the Civil War loomed, the city celebrated St. Joseph's Night with masked balls (with the condition that all attendees had to unmask before a committee before entering). That year, the Young Men's Benevolent Association hosted a fancy dress and masked ball at Odd Fellows' Hall, and the New Lusitanos Benevolent Association—either a Portuguese group or a society named after the horse breed—held one at its hall. A roster listed in an earlier advertisement determines that the New Lusitanos Benevolent Association's members included white men from various ethnic backgrounds.[114] However, a different kind of event was held at the Union Hall: a calico ball. The advertisement promised that "this being St. Joseph's Day, or *Mi-Carême,* all these balls will be scenes of the greatest festivity, and merrious devotion to Terpsichore and Momus."[115]

Calico balls had become a craze in the northern states, allegedly after a ball was given in New York City in 1855 by a wealthy woman to help the less fortunate. The rich women wore simple, inexpensive dresses made of calico to the ball and donated them after the party to those in need. The idea took off and spread throughout the country. Even New Orleans showed interest when, apparently, an advertisement for a non-St. Joseph's Day ball in 1861 explained that several years earlier, a calico ball was given at the Union Hall, where "no ladies were admitted in any other dress than that of plain calico, or without having passed an ordeal of necessary scrutiny as to character, by the invitation committee. The ladies on this occasion will have to leave their muslins and silks at home and appear on a perfect equality as to dress. The cheapest kind of dress at that."[116] That "ordeal of scrutiny" might have been an attempt to deny admittance to women of mixed race.

On March 15, 1862, instead of advertisements for balls on St. Joseph's Day, an order from the Confederate States of America announced that martial law was in effect in Orleans Parish and the neighboring parishes of Jefferson, St. Bernard, and Plaquemines. All white males were required to pledge allegiance to the Confederacy and to carry Confederate passports.[117] A month after the announcement of martial law and one year into the Civil War, Union forces took control of New Orleans. By 1863, masked balls were prohibited, even on St. Joseph's Night.

4

OCCUPATION, RECONSTRUCTION, AND BEYOND

Carnival Is Crowned King of New Orleans

St. Joseph's night is certainly one of the greatest ball nights of the year. It fairly rivals Mardi Gras in its pleasures and temptations.

—*Daily Picayune,* March 20, 1874

Almost every hall in town is engaged, and the balls will probably be the centres of attraction.

—*Daily Picayune,* March 19, 1881

To-night is St. Joseph's night, and it will be almost universally observed by clubs and associations throughout the city. Dances and entertainments will fill practically every dance hall in the city, and the merry-making will extend from the Barracks to Carrollton.

—*Daily Picayune,* March 19, 1903

By May 1, 1862, New Orleans was firmly under Union control. General Benjamin Butler's headquarters were established at the St. Charles Hotel, a site that had previously hosted St. Joseph's Day balls in the American part of town. After an unruly group took down the American flag from the US Mint, Butler decided to act quickly by arresting, convicting, and hanging William Bruce Mumford on June 7, 1862, for treason. Butler also issued the notorious General Order No. 28, also known as the "Women's Order," which stated that any woman found guilty of insulting or showing contempt for officers could be "treated as a woman of the town plying her avocation." These actions set the tone for the turbulent years of Union control of the city.[1]

In the fall of 1862, the Union army implemented a pass system for all Black New Orleanians, and by 1864, a nighttime curfew was also in place for Black residents.[2] Enforcing these regulations proved challenging because many Union soldiers found the racial ambiguity of New Orleans's population confusing; as one Union soldier remarked, "It is hard telling who is white here."[3] Many families, both Black and white, had "ancestors in the other race," an anomaly not seen elsewhere in the United States. These new rules diminished the position of Creoles of color, which were further constrained after the failure of Reconstruction in 1877.

Yet the people of New Orleans were not going to give up their festivities because of the war, so the military mayor set up a system of permits to allow parties and gatherings. In a large bound book filled with delicate script on onionskin paper, permits were issued for various celebrations, from children's birthday parties to St. Joseph's Day balls.[4] Despite the absence of newspaper ads for St. Joseph's Day events in 1864 or 1865, more than 150 mandatory permits were issued by the acting military mayor for balls, private parties, and soirees between January 1 and March 12, 1864.[5]

New Orleans's quick surrender to Union forces saved it from the destruction that many other southern towns suffered, enabling a quick return to relative normality. During the war years, theaters remained open, and balls continued to be held on St. Joseph's Day; they were promoted as grand fancy dress balls, but attendees had to remain unmasked. Contemporary accounts suggest that most parties were small, but that there were some larger private balls that had to be shut down for lacking permits; no Confederate sympathizers would "humiliate themselves by going to our masters [Union officers] to ask permission to dance in their own parlors."[6] Because most balls "were attended by federal troops in uniform and the women of the

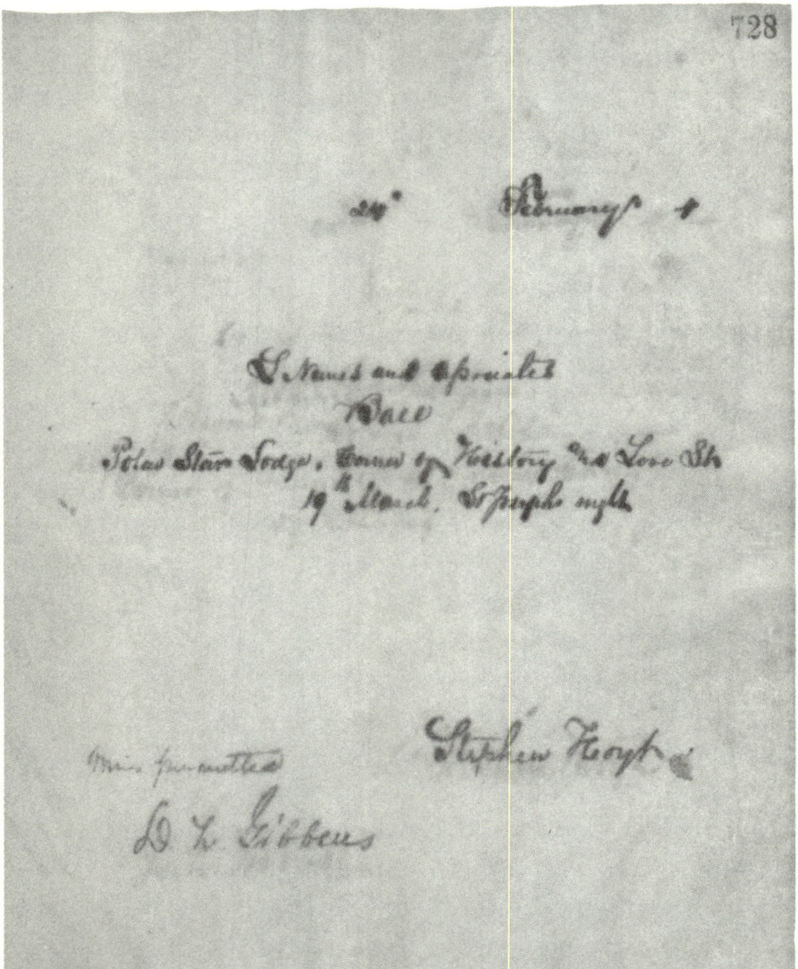
728

24 February

Ball

Polar Star Lodge, Corner of History and Love Sts

19th March, St Joseph's night

Stephen Hoyt

D. L. Gibbens

Civil War military mayor's book of permit requests from 1864 with a permit for a St. Joseph's Night ball at the Polar Star Lodge at the corner of History and Love Streets for March 19, 1864. New Orleans (La.), Office of the Mayor, AA670, City Archives & Special Collections, New Orleans Public Library.

town," some white New Orleanians did express their hostility toward Union occupation by boycotting the balls.[7] Still, most Black New Orleanians felt differently about the occupiers.

In 1864, the practice of masking had been officially banned, possibly due to concerns that the anonymity provided by wearing masks facilitated criminal activity. Yet, on March 8, 1866, an advertisement in the *Daily Picayune* indicated that, after the war, masking, a key element of Creole celebrations, was again permitted. It read:

> Ball Costumes.—Everything pertaining to a complete outfit for a fancy or masquerade ball, can always be procured at the well-known establishment of M'me Groux, 93 Conti St. Her assortment of masks, dominoes and costumes is very fine, and her store has long been the resort of the votaries of terpsichore. The Madame hints that it is her intention to visit the French capital during the approaching summer, and her return may be looked upon as the advent of everything that is new and novel in character ball costumes.

The advertisement ran the day before St. Joseph's Day, perhaps to catch the eye of someone preparing for a big mid-Lent party. The promise of French-made masks and costumes, an obvious selling point, reflected the continuing French influence on the residents' celebrations. But French influence extended beyond fashion, with the Young Men's Society promoting that "the fashionables of Paris are introducing the promenade concert at their grand balls, to give a diversity of dancing, and to amuse those who don't care about dancing" and adding that it will be "inaugurated" at its ball on St. Joseph's Night at Odd Fellows' Hall. Interestingly, its ball was advertised as a "calico ball, being the first of its kind in a long time." The same night, falling in line with tradition, Fire Company No. 24 held a masked ball at the Masonic Hall.[8]

Also in 1866, a newspaper article about a calico ball (see chapter 3) held at Godchaux's Hall in January described why this northern-inspired ball was popular after the war, noting that it was an American alternative to costuming and masking: "People have not the means to give and keep up splendid balls, and those who attempt to get them up will strike the first blow at all amusements of this kind in the parish. It is particularly the duty of those who have ample means to appear at balls in costly dresses, to adopt the calico arrangement on such occasions."[9]

At this time, an estimated four-fifths of the total population belonged to at least one mutual aid and benevolent society: both Black and white New Orleanians found comfort and camaraderie in these groups.[10] These groups included orphan aid and benevolent associations, social and literary clubs, militia groups, Masonic organizations, racial improvement associations, and even baseball clubs.[11] St. Joseph's Day balls provided excellent fundraising opportunities, and these events continued to thrive. The white planter elites' perceived loss of power and wealth after the defeat of the Confederacy and during the era of Reconstruction led to the expansion, organization, and privatization of balls in New Orleans to publicly demonstrate that civil authority had returned to their hands.

In 1867, St. Joseph's Day inspired at least two balls in the city, both masked, with one called "the mi-careme ball of St. Joseph"; one ball was held at the French Opera House, requiring the cancellation of performances of the French Dramatic Company.[12] In 1868, three grand masked and fancy dress balls were held on St. Joseph's Night. One was held at the New Opera House after that evening's performance, and two were staged in the American part of town: one at the National Theatre, a German theater, and another at the Olympic Theatre on St. Charles Street. In 1869, a newspaper article noted that there were "quite a number of balls to-night, all of which will be largely attended, occurring, as they do, on this special festival—an oasis, so to speak, in the long lenten season."[13]

The following year, St. Joseph's Night was promoted as an opportunity to "see New Orleans *en masque,* and be present at a mask ball such as is given in our city during the Carnival. . . . ; the managers of this ball are the same gentlemen who undertook the arrangements for Mardi Gras night at this theatre, which is a sure indication that the affair will be in every respect as brilliant as that which closed the Carnival."[14] Thus, Mardi Gras, St. Joseph's Night, and masking were still seen as interconnected.

New Orleans's thriving postbellum social life caught many visitors by surprise. In 1871, a young woman proclaimed that every night there were "balls, parties, and dinners" often lasting until two or three o'clock in the morning and that she was "almost tired of it."[15] Alfred Waud, who during the Civil War provided illustrations for newspapers, made a detailed drawing of a St. Joseph's Night ball, titled "St. Louis Ball, N.O." It shows a lavish room with masked and costumed dancers frolicking under blazing chandeliers.[16]

Reconstruction and its political turmoil did little to thwart balls and parties, even though attempts were made to limit them. As Christopher

Artistic rendering of a room filled with masked dancers, titled "St. Louis Ball, N.O." and inscribed "St. Joseph's Night Ball, New Orleans." Drawing by Alfred Waud, 1871. Alfred R. Waud Collection, The Historic New Orleans Collection.

Benfey points out, "bad years tend to inspire good carnivals; the worse the times, the greater the need for escape and oblivion." Reconstruction inspired "good carnivals" for the insecure white elites of New Orleans, enabling parades and pageantry to thrive.[17]

Yet, during those years, non-Creole white people with money and power began to exert greater control over Carnival as New Orleans became a tourist destination. Whether watching the Mardi Gras parades in the streets or attending a ball, these visitors became an integral part of Carnival's growth.

Those Americans who made New Orleans their home established their own neighborhoods and "began to either dictate or discard the French and Spanish customs of the city."[18] Carnival gradually became transformed into an Anglo-American celebration. Carnival merged with the debutante tradition, serving as the unofficial debut for many elite uptown Anglo women. It also became used as a vehicle to reinforce the racial and social hierarchy. The white krewes used the "spectacle of street parades to instill terror in blacks and recent European immigrants,"[19] while "Krewesmen established themselves as the patriarchal rulers of New Orleans society."[20] Edgar Degas visited the city during Reconstruction and found that the town was "Janus-faced. . . . One secret society plotted festivity while another plotted terrorism," revealing the "two conspiracies—the Mistick Krewe of Comus and the Crescent City White League—mixed methods, personnel, and locales."[21] Emerging from the perceived stress of sharing power and witnessing progress for people of color, some Anglo New Orleanians, fueled by hatred and fear, hijacked the Carnival season, eventually leading to the birth of modern Mardi Gras with the Krewe of Comus in 1857.[22]

In other parts of the world where slavery had ended, "Carnival was taken over by the freed people while former masters avoided the streets." In contrast, in New Orleans, former enslavers organized Carnival to make it "safe" for tourists to travel and enjoy this holiday. "New Orleans Mardi Gras in its modern form was thus a child of Reconstruction and counterreaction," and tourism quickly became a new source of wealth for the white elites in the city.[23]

Although postwar New Orleans became more diverse in terms of religion and ethnicity, the city's Catholic roots remained strong and intact. Protestants participated in Catholic-related holidays, so that "the Mardi Gras carnival grew into the most significant public event in the annual calendar."[24]

However, Samuel Kinser claims that it was the participation of non-Catholics that enabled Mardi Gras to thrive. It resulted in a "de-Catholicization of the Lent–Carnival relationship," which was necessary for "Carnival to become Mardi Gras." Carnival behavior became "disconnected from religious behavior by the gradually growing interest of Protestants in the balls and parades and by the urge to do more than observe." The process of "de-Catholicization" contributed to the longevity and mass appeal of celebrations like Mardi Gras and St. Joseph's Day. They were no longer specific markers of French Catholicism: all New Orleanians celebrated these occasions regardless of race, religion, or heritage.

Yet not everyone appreciated the contributions of those non-Catholics, as Kinser discovered in this newspaper article:

> In the early days of our city, when it was peopled by a Catholic community who understood and could appreciate the observance of the day, Mardi Gras was a season of striking and memorable peculiarities. Then people of an elevated rank took part in the processions, long lines of carriages, filled with gaily dressed masquers, troops of revelers, decked in costumes representing every nationality and filling through the streets in glittering throngs. . . . But now the aspect of things have changed. Our population is not what it was. The old regime is no more. It has fallen into the list of forgotten things, and the sway over manners has passed to the swine-eating Saxon.[25]

Before the war, some masked balls on St. Joseph's Day had used their proceeds to benefit specific charities, but most were open to the public. Advertisements for St. Joseph's Day balls held after the war revealed the onset of a more segregated city. By the 1870s, "socially exclusive balls were instituted."[26]

For instance, in 1871, the De Blanc Zouaves,[27] "5th Reg. Louisiana Volunteer, Militia" hosted a "military, fancy dress, and calico ball" at Carroll Hall on Elysian Fields.[28] A lack of information about this group has led to speculation that it may have been one of the numerous paramilitary organizations, similar to the White League, that emerged in New Orleans during that period. The reference to De Blanc is an important clue. Jean Maximilien Alcibiades Derneville DeBlanc from St. Mary's Parish was a Confederate colonel believed to be the founder of Louisiana's version of the Ku Klux Klan, the Knights of the White Camellia, in 1867. There were also rumors that he led the Knights after relocating to New Orleans in June 1874. On May 3, 1873, he led 600 men in St. Martinville, Louisiana, in a demonstration to contest the governor's election; two Metropolitan policemen died when it turned violent; the Metropolitan was a mixed-race law enforcement agency formed during Reconstruction. Although he was put on trial in New Orleans for inciting violence, DeBlanc was greeted by a cheering crowd. Even after being charged under the Enforcement Act of 1871 for "intimidating Negroes," he later was appointed to the Louisiana Supreme Court. These terrorist organizations altered the social landscape of the city, particularly with the Battle of Liberty Place,[29] when the White League sought to overthrow the Republican-led government in 1874.

Social life in New Orleans was disrupted for a year or two when the Panic of 1873 struck the city and the Colfax Massacre, in which dozens of freed Blacks were killed, occurred on Easter Sunday.[30] Earlier that year, Edward King, a reporter for *Scribner's Monthly,* noticed that during Carnival "white and black join in the masquerading," but claimed that "the Americans masquerade grimly. There is little of that wild luxuriance of fun in the streets of New Orleans which has made Italian cities so famous; people go to their sports with an air of pride, but not of all-pervading enjoyment."[31] Perhaps this was a premonition of what was to come.

In 1874, the legislature attempted to restrict the observance of a festive Sabbath by passing the Sunday Closing Law. The law was soon nullified when the attorney general claimed that "it was not legally enacted, and that was that."[32] This was an example of Catholic traditions triumphing over

Protestant Anglo-American rules. However, the Americans soon discovered that these exotic celebrations, including St. Joseph's Day, could be lucrative. The *Daily Picayune* proclaimed St. Joseph's Night as a second Mardi Gras, giving people an opportunity to see a version of the world-famous Carnival in New Orleans. The St. Joseph's Night ball at the Opera House "was a genuine resurrection of the carnival—a continuation of the carnival's unfinished fun . . . Even 'Carnival' entertainment stretched beyond that of Carnival."[33] By enticing tourists to visit the city at times other than Mardi Gras, St. Joseph's Night celebrations increased the tourist trade.[34]

Civic and social organizations like the Silver Bell Social Club were praised for hosting popular balls "on every ball night—St. Joseph, New Year's Eve, and Mardi Gras," further illustrating the significance of St. Joseph's Day in the city's calendar of social events. Not only did white New Orleans celebrate St. Joseph's Day but also in the Black community, "the last masked balls of the season were usually held on St. Joseph's Eve (March 18) at Geddes, Globe, Economy, Union, and other halls," with masquerade parties lasting until the early morning hours.[35]

For example, the Société d'Économie et d'Assistance Mutuelle, a mutual aid and benevolent society founded in 1836 by and for elite free people of color, decided to build a hall after hosting its first charity ball at the rented Washington Ballroom in 1841. Encouraged by the substantial profits from that event, the group built Economy Hall, which was completed after more than a decade of construction in 1857.[36] The public ballroom featured a tongue-and-groove floor, a musicians' balcony, a first loge with box seats, a ladies' dressing parlor, and an apartment upstairs for the *gardienne,* "the female caretaker of the hall who also sold gumbo, pâté, and liquor before and after the meetings."[37]

The St. Joseph's Day ball at Economy Hall was one of the Société's most popular and profitable events. Fatima Shaik discovered in her family's records that in 1872, "the committee in charge of the St. Joseph's ball spent $142, including $63 for liquor and $36 for music, but the dance generated $123 at the door and a $120 profit from the sale of food and drinks—almost seven weeks of work for a Louisiana carpenter." The money raised during the evening's festivities was "a hefty sum for the nuns, the orphanage, and tuition for the colored children at the Couvent School." By the 1880s, their St. Joseph's balls were "second in popularity only to Mardi Gras celebrations."[38]

At the Perfect Union Hall, home of the New Lusitanos Benevolent Association, "ladies of Portuguese descent" reportedly danced for hours to compensate for the Lenten days of penance, explaining that "St. Joseph's night is certainly one of the greatest ball nights of the year. It fairly rivals Mardi Gras in its pleasures and temptations. Falling as it does in the middle of Lent, it serves as a sort of wayside oasis to those persons whose pleasure-loving disposition makes it difficult for them to fast from dancing for the whole allotted forty days." Balls served as vehicles for benevolent societies "to increase the treasury and usefulness," and the "oldest and most successful" such association in the city "boasted" of being a ball-giving association.[39]

In postbellum New Orleans, the conflict was no longer one of Creoles versus Americans but rather Black versus white. During the Civil War, white Creoles and Americans "learned to fight together; they used the years of Reconstruction to conspire together." In fact, among the leaders of the Battle of Liberty Place was Michel Musson, a prominent Creole businessman. The transition from tripartite to biracial dynamics in the city was nearly complete, leading to a "violent unraveling of human relations that had taken a century to weave."[40]

During Reconstruction, race relations in New Orleans "swung like a crazy pendulum back and forth between integration and segregation," as some businesses allowed integration while neighboring establishments—including churches—were reserved for whites only. The city's rules had no rhyme or reason.[41] However, they permitted interracial marriages and outlawed segregation not only in schools but also in public places.

As Daniel Brook notes, "postwar federal occupation would complete the long-delayed Americanization" of New Orleans.[42] Ironically, the year the Louisiana legislature declared Mardi Gras a legal holiday, Carnival celebrations in New Orleans were canceled due to the attempted coup at Liberty Place the previous September.[43] By March, balls had resumed on St. Joseph's Day, including one organized by the Violet Social Club, a Black women's organization. Although not officially called a masked ball, the *Daily Picayune* described it as "a delightful Terpsichorean entertainment at Stonewall Jackson Hall," where attendees were "votaries and admirers of Mi-Careme."[44] The "Constitution of the Violet Social Club of the Seventh District of New Orleans, Louisiana" confirmed that the club was established "for enjoyments such as given balls." "Any person who shall be of a good and moral character, respectable person, may become a member of this Club, on paying an entrance fee of twenty-five cents, and monthly fee of ten cents."[45]

In 1877, Reconstruction officially ended: it was a complete failure, leaving the city's population more divided than ever before. As K. Stephen Prince explains,

> In the aftermath of Reconstruction, white Southerners revolutionized their region's racial order. They engineered a retreat from the racial egalitarianism of the post-Civil War years, stripping away the civil and political rights that African Americans had earned in the wake of emancipation. The system of discrimination and domination they built would come to be known as Jim Crow. Beginning with the segregation of the region's railways in the 1880s, white southerners systematically drew the color line through the region's public space.[46]

After Reconstruction ended, the Southern white elite regained some of their power by asserting their influence over newer white transplants. As more northerners moved to New Orleans, they were greeted by social ostracism, rather than physical violence. They realized that to thrive in the city they needed to comply with its prevailing political, religious, and social practices: their compliance exacerbated the growing racism and social divisions that emerged as Reconstruction faltered.[47] Even the Catholic Church aligned with the rest of the nation's racial traditions, abandoning the three-tiered system it created during the colonial era. The era of Jim Crow loomed on the horizon.

Yet nighttime masked balls remained popular, accompanied by additional "military observances."[48] Military parades, followed by military balls, contrasted sharply with the mirthful masquerades from day to night, as announced in a headline in the *Daily Picayune:* "How the Soldiers and the Dancers Will Observe the Anniversary."[49]

In 1878, Tiro al Bersaglio ("Hit the Target"), an Italian sharpshooters group founded in 1868 and incorporated in 1869, held a procession followed by a dinner to honor the famous Italian general Giuseppe [Joseph] Garibaldi on St. Joseph's Day. This group was one of the few legally recognized militia organizations in the state of Louisiana. For many Catholics, celebrating a saint's feast day that coincides with one's name is a cherished tradition. In the same year, two military balls took place: one at Grunewald Hall for the First Company, Cazadores de Orleans, a volunteer militia of Spanish American men formed in 1847 under the Louisiana Legion that disbanded in 1862, and another at St. Patrick's Hall for the Gardes Lafayette. In the following years, military balls flourished, alongside dances for benevolent societies, many of which were linked to workers' groups, such as the butchers of New Orleans, who gathered at Grunewald Hall for a ball on St. Joseph's Day. They had "enough of the French blood about them to make all their balls, and especially their masked balls, pleasant and enjoyable," emphasizing that the ball catered to the non-Anglo-American working class.[50]

Mardi Gras came to be marketed as a fun event, and by 1880, an estimated 60,000 tourists were visiting the city annually to celebrate it. By 1900, that number ballooned to 100,000, and the town was reimagined as a tourist destination, with Mardi Gras as its main attraction. Travel writer George Sala confirmed that on Ash Wednesday, "the process of depopulation was visible to a phenomenal extent at all the hotels" and that "huge mountains of luggage were piled up in the rotunda of the St. Charles (hotel)" as the tourists abandoned the city.

New Orleans was wild and lascivious but safe, thanks to the control of the white elites.[51] Sala also noted that Mardi Gras and mid-Lent attracted non-Catholic participation. He observed that there was

> some difficulty on the Wednesday and Thursday succeeding Mardi Gras, in convincing the good people of New Orleans that the Carnival was over,

> that Lent had begun, and that Fun was as dead as Queen Anne. On the French side of Canal-street the Creoles, being orthodox Romanists, meekly accepted the inevitable, furled their flags, laid by their masks, and made up their minds for forty days' abstinence from gaiety and conviviality:—to be alleviated perchance by a trifling "spurt" of music and dancing at the Mi-carême.

The Anglo-American population of the city "seemed generally unaware of the propriety of fasting and mourning in sackcloth and ashes."[52] Those who were not Catholic did not grasp the significance of Mardi Gras as an end to festivities: because they were not required to give anything up for Lent, they saw no reason not to continue the celebration. An article from the 1930s explained how Catholics observed Lent in New Orleans: "Forty days begin a time of privations and promises which were faithfully kept you would abstain during these forty days from sweets, or from going to any place of amusement. The meals were rather frugal: meats and fish were forbidden at the same meal, only one full meal was allowed, with the exception of Sundays, which day was not considered Lent, as well as the 19th of March (St. Joseph's day, which is generally mid-lent)." Young girls were to avoid their "sweethearts," "abstain from sweets or anything they liked most," and not read any novels.[53]

Another way that the American residents differed from Creoles was their overt, public focus on the bottom line. Alice Dunbar-Nelson, a Creole poet and journalist born in New Orleans in 1875 to a white seaman and a formerly enslaved seamstress, addressed the crude business-only mindset of the Anglo-Americans that annoyed Creoles in her short story, "M'Sieu Fortier's Violin." One character expressed horror on hearing that an American had replaced a Creole as opera manager. "Bah! These English-speaking people could do nothing unless there was a trust, a syndicate, a company immense and dishonest. It was going to be a guaranteed business, with a strictly financial basis."[54] Discretion in Creole New Orleans was especially valued in money and social situations.

Even one of the oldest professions that certainly depended on discre-

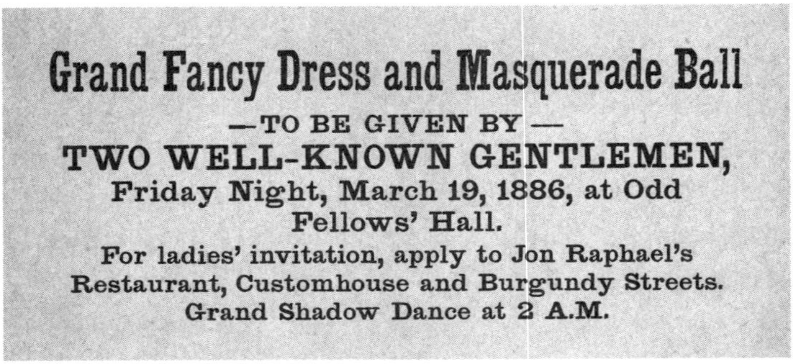

Grand Fancy Dress and Masquerade Ball
—TO BE GIVEN BY—
TWO WELL-KNOWN GENTLEMEN,
Friday Night, March 19, 1886, at Odd Fellows' Hall.
For ladies' invitation, apply to Jon Raphael's Restaurant, Customhouse and Burgundy Streets.
Grand Shadow Dance at 2 A.M.

Newspaper advertisement for a masquerade ball on March 19, 1886, *New Orleans Times-Picayune,* March 18, 1886.

tion, prostitution, sponsored masked balls on St. Joseph's Day. In 1886, a masked ball was advertised as being presented by "Two Well-Known Gentlemen" at Odd Fellows' Hall.[55] These "Two Well-Known Gentlemen" were likely Tom Anderson and Frank Lamothe, who owned several brothels and bars in Storyville, the legal red-light district in New Orleans established in 1897, and that thrived until prostitution was outlawed in 1917. This ball was probably one of their earlier "notorious *bal masques*" of "infamous revelries."[56]

By 1886, the concept of who was considered Creole had become Americanized. Skin color, rather than ethnicity, became the key criterion: to join the Creole Association of Louisiana, one only needed to be of white descent, and French or Spanish ancestry was no longer required.[57]

Before the public and private masked balls on St. Joseph's Day faded into a lost New Orleans tradition, a krewe that had paraded alongside the early pantheon of Carnival groups, the Independent Order of the Moon, made a surprise appearance. On March 19, 1886, this krewe restaged its parade originally held on Mardi Gras Day "to burlesque the Carnival, the procession being styled 'A Carnival Wake.'" After marching through crowded streets, the krewe hosted a masked ball at Exposition Hall.[58]

Founded in 1881, the Independent Order of the Moon (IOOHM) parade took place on Mardi Gras until 1888, except for 1885 when they "just didn't show up."[59] According to the *Times-Picayune,* the highlights of the Carnival included the "magnificent pageant of Rex, grotesque displays of the Phunny Phorty Phellows and the Independent Order of the Moon."[60] There is no record of whether they appeared in any other year, so this was likely a unique affair.

In 1886 as well, an even greater luminary, the King of Carnival, Rex, celebrated St. Joseph's Day with an exclusive gathering. The ball is described in *A Girl's Life in New Orleans: The Diary of Ella Grunewald, 1884–1886,* edited by Hans Rasmussen. Ella, the daughter of the man who built Grunewald Hall, refers to March 19 as St. Joseph's Day and records that on that day, "I went to Rex's ball with Papa & Mamma, our whole family was there & I had a perfectly lovely time, we did not get home until one o'clock, I felt awfully guilty while there, as it was Lent."[61] Ella felt guilty about attending a ball during Lent, perhaps because she did not acknowledge its connection to St. Joseph's Day and mid-Lent.

A newspaper article that mentioned this ball also noted that "the Royal Host" was to "repeat on St. Joseph's Night, March 19, the pageant of Mardi Gras, but Carnival enthusiasm has been so feeble this year the idea was relinquished. *The Royal Host* will give, however, a ball in the French Opera House to their friends."[62] According to Rex historian and archivist Stephen Hales, the Royal Host were the Dukes of the Realm, an elite segment of the organization that paid higher dues and enjoyed additional privileges.

However, the smaller private ball must have been a success because a year later, on March 16, 1887, it was announced that "Rex held his reception on the night of Mardi Gras, but Carnival Court will give a midlent ball on Saturday, 19th inst., at the French Opera House, which will be a very brilliant event. The invitations are now being issued." They were sent to all the members of Rex. The next day, the *Daily Picayune* reported details of the event. Nine hundred guests attended the ball, which was adorned with decorations in the royal colors of Carnival—purple, green, and gold. Although it was not a masquerade ball, the riding members of the krewe, along with the King of Carnival and his pages, were allowed to wear their costumes one more time for the event. It is noteworthy to point that the ball was

Admit card (front and back) for a mid-Lent ball hosted by the Krewe of Rex at the French Opera House, March 19, 1887. Reproduced courtesy of the School of Design of the Krewe of Rex Organization.

announced as a mid-Lent event and was not referred to as St. Joseph's Day, possibly to avoid an affiliation with Creoles.

For a while, St. Joseph's Day balls continued as masked affairs, much to the delight of the people of New Orleans. In 1888, the *Daily Picayune* referred to St. Joseph's Day as "le petit carnival," proclaiming, "When the carnival is ended, and the ashes and sack cloth [*sic*] are the order of the day, pleasure seekers look to St. Joseph's Night—mid-Lent—with great anxiety and interest. The occasion is always celebrated in grand style by balls, *soiree dansantes* and parties."[63]

Yet despite the popularity of its "midlent ball," Rex never held another one outside the Carnival season. Perhaps this decision might have contributed to the belief that St. Joseph's Day was not meant for the elites who belonged to the now-popular Carnival krewes.

By excluding St. Joseph's Day from the traditions then associated solely with Carnival, the white elite of krewes such as Comus, Momus, and Rex maintained their dominance over Mardi Gras, reflecting their control of the city following the Civil War.[64] Sociologist Kevin Fox Gotham observes that when "old-line krewes established rationalized and exclusive parades and balls," the racial divide was promoted as a form of "local authenticity,"[65] and the formerly public balls evolved into "private rituals" of the white elites of New Orleans.[66] This new Carnival emerged from an aristocracy eager to reassert power lost after the war by staging a theatrical reminder that they remained in charge of the city. The theme of Comus's first parade was "aggressively English in its celebration of what New Orleans had always considered a French festival. It is hard to think of a clearer assertion than this parade that the lead in the holiday had passed from French speakers to Anglo-Americans" and that "Carnival in its organized form was the product of white reaction."[67]

This new Carnival spirit still mocked the faux regal displays of the wealthy and powerful, but "it was the genius of the New Orleans social order that the permissible mimicry of upper-class whites served only to legitimize the hierarchy, by encouraging subalterns to recognize their place even as they temporarily escape it."[68] Thus, "Carnival in New Orleans . . . dramatizes the segregation of people, or better, confirms in the festival a separation to which the daily world testifies but the ideological creed categorically denies."[69] White elites in New Orleans quickly realized that they could exploit Carnival for profit, just as they had long manipulated the commercial sector in the city by creating a space of superiority.

White outsiders participated in Carnival festivities, while New Orleanians of different social classes or racial backgrounds were often excluded.[70] Tourists and visitors were more likely to receive invitations to a ball than most natives, as George Sala discovered when he was "the honored recipient of two heart-shaped cards of invitation, gorgeously printed in silver and colours, and enclosed in hotpressed envelopes decorated with costly monograms, to the Sixth Representation of the Knights of Momus at the Grand Opera House on the 5th of February next."[71]

Rex's influence reached far and wide, and many believed that "recovery from the war required the revitalization of Carnival."[72] Advertisements for Rex were spotted outside the city; for example, Sala found an official proclamation from the Rex organization in Atlanta, in which the King of Carnival "announced the commencement of his reign, and amicably, but sternly, demanded all railway companies within his jurisdiction provide transportation at reduced rates for his loyal subjects bent on enjoying the delirious festivities of Mardi Gras in the Crescent City."[73]

With the transformation of Carnival from "an unorganized and informal street revel into an entire social season, a highly stylized program of balls and pageants, related to debutantes and a caste system as rigid, although in a different way, as that of the Creoles," the number of St. Joseph's Day balls declined, and the tone of the celebrations began to shift toward the end of the nineteenth century. Masked balls started to disappear, replaced by dances and soirees. In an article titled "An Oasis in the Social Desert," the Euterpe Benevolent Association's masquerade ball (also listed as a calico ball) was held at Perfect Union Hall on Rampart Street near Dumaine. Heading uptown, the Pythian Hall Association returned for its second annual fancy-dress ball without mentioning masks. A dance benefit was held at the Eagle's Nest, located in the French Quarter, to raise funds for new uniforms for the Golden Eagle No. 6. The American Athletic Club celebrated with a "gymnastic exhibition and dance" at their hall across the river in Gretna. The Jefferson Guards hosted a "grand ball and competitive drill," and a "night's affair" took place at the Odd Fellows' Hall.[74]

An unusual notice titled "St. Joseph's Day" also appeared in 1895. It described an alleged traditional practice in which Creole girls engaged to find a husband, connecting it to the feast day rather than to mid-Lent. The young Catholic women pray "nine days during the novena at St. Joseph's shrine" asking, "Who the coming man may be?"[75] However, the *Daily Picayune* also reported that "St. Joseph's day, or 'Mi Careme,' as the Creoles term it, is always a gala night in the French quarter. Notwithstanding the condemnation of Mother Church, the happy Latin nature asserts itself, and the Creoles will dance and sing and make merry at the 'Mi Careme.'"[76] This article connected St. Joseph's Day to mid-Lent, suggesting that it remained a Creole celebration observed by individuals of "Latin" heritage.

In 1896, the landmark Supreme Court decision *Plessy v. Ferguson* dealt another blow to people of color in New Orleans by erasing much of the in-between spaces that Creoles of color had established and further degrading their social status.[77] Jim Crow laws were not only intended to segregate Blacks and whites but also enabled white control. "There was always a middle stratum between the white city and the black city, shared spaces through which both black and white residents moved regularly," and masked balls were one such common space where "interracial contact—even a limited form of interracial sociability—survived and thrived."[78] Given that balls on St. Joseph's Day were often masked and not under the control of Anglo New Orleans, such anxieties may have contributed to the demise of the costumed balls that were once so prevalent on this night.

That year, for instance, alongside two masquerade balls were three that were not masked. The American Athletic Club hosted an "attractive hop," the Washington Circle, "a social organization composed of well known young men gave a fancy dress ball," and the Ladies' Concord Benevolent Association "gave a very attractive ball."[79]

By 1898, only three balls were mentioned in the newspaper, and none were masked.[80] In 1900, a few parties or receptions took place, including a fancy dress and calico ball and a "fancy dress and masquerade party" hosted by the Pink Carnation Social Club at the "dancing pavilion" on Customhouse Street.[81] In 1901, a single article described a "fancy dress reception" hosted by the Old Ramblers' Club. A surprise nighttime parade rolled out from the ball, though it remains unclear whether it was costumed. The group, known as the Knights of Joy, organized a "street parade of handsomely decorated carriages," complete with a king passing through the French Quarter to his coronation ball at the Perfect Union Hall.[82] Although the parade occurred on March 19, no reason was provided for the festivities, and neither St. Joseph nor mid-Lent was mentioned.

In 1903, the Società Italiana di Mutua Beneficenza San Giuseppe (St. Joseph Mutual Benefit Society) hosted its first St. Joseph's ball. It was not a masquerade, and it took place after a high mass, although there was no mention of what would become the symbol of modern Sicilian celebrations of St. Joseph's Day in New Orleans: the altar. Meanwhile, the *Daily Picayune* claimed, "Tonight is St. Joseph's night, and it will be almost universally observed by clubs and associations throughout the city. Dances and entertainments will fill practically every hall in the city, and the merry making will extend from the Barracks to Carrollton"; however, only two of these celebrations were masquerade balls.[83]

In 1904, the Sisters of St. Joseph decorated the altar at their chapel on St. Philip and Galvez Streets with palms, ferns, Easter lilies, and numerous

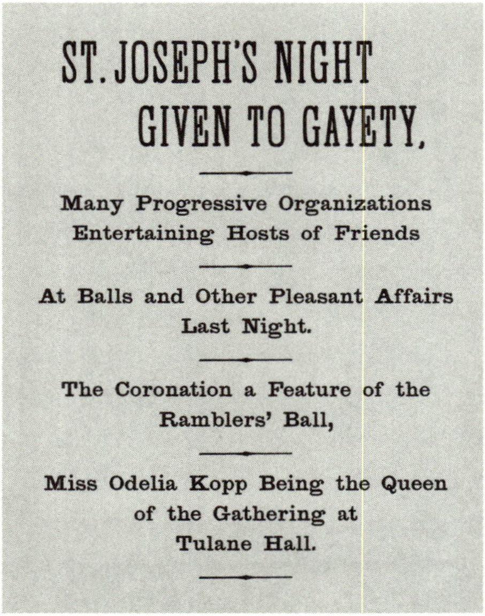
ST. JOSEPH'S NIGHT
GIVEN TO GAYETY.

Many Progressive Organizations
Entertaining Hosts of Friends

At Balls and Other Pleasant Affairs
Last Night.

The Coronation a Feature of the
Ramblers' Ball,

Miss Odelia Kopp Being the Queen
of the Gathering at
Tulane Hall.

St. Joseph's Night advertisement, *New Orleans Times-Picayune,* March 20, 1903.

candles. For an added effect, electric lights encircled the statue of the saint as a tribute on his feast day as the "patron saint of the universal church." However, this day was dedicated to solemn devotion, beginning at 6:30 a.m. with a low mass, followed by a high mass at 8:30 a.m., complete with music and twenty altar boys dressed in white and red robes. The day concluded with a sermon and benediction at 5 p.m.[84]

Once again, the Italian St. Joseph Mutual Benefit Society had a ball at the Pythian Hall on St. Joseph's Eve "for the benefit of the relief fund" and continued celebrating the next day. At 10:30 a.m., a high mass was celebrated at St. Alphonsus Church, followed by a procession and banquet. In the afternoon, the Italian and American flags were blessed.[85]

On November 30, 1906, a newspaper contained a "SPECIAL NOTICE—BIDS FOR THE rental of the dancing hall of the Masonic and Odd Fellows' Hall Association, Limited, 1116 Perdido Street, for Lundi Gras and St. Joseph's Nights will be sold to the highest bidder on Saturday, Dec. 1, 1906, at 7:30 p.m." This revealed the competition to secure ballrooms for St. Joseph's Night. However, that the hall was still available and not yet rented for St. Joseph's Day perhaps signaled that St. Joseph's Day balls were not as popular as they once were.[86]

St. Joseph's Day in New Orleans continued to be celebrated throughout the early 1900s, with varied entertainment. There was a "fancy dress ball" for the Roebuck Club at Odd Fellows' Hall, another at Olympic Hall for the members of the Lion Social Club, and a "fancy dress reception" at Washington Artillery Hall for the Rosebud Club. An unusual celebration was held at the Stag Athletic Club. The members held their first "grand complimentary masquerade and fancy dress ball" at their hall from 8:30 p.m. until midnight, after which "a single hour will be devoted to a catch-as-catch-can wrestling match," followed by more dancing.[87]

The Eagles at Home hosted a mid-Lent "hop" at their venue on Bourbon Street to raise funds for their tomb, while the Directoire Social Club held one of the "largest attended balls of the night in Odd Fellows' Hall" without mentioning masks. Local Lodge No. 54, Brotherhood of Railway Clerks, organized an "excursion" to celebrate the night on the steamer *J. S.*

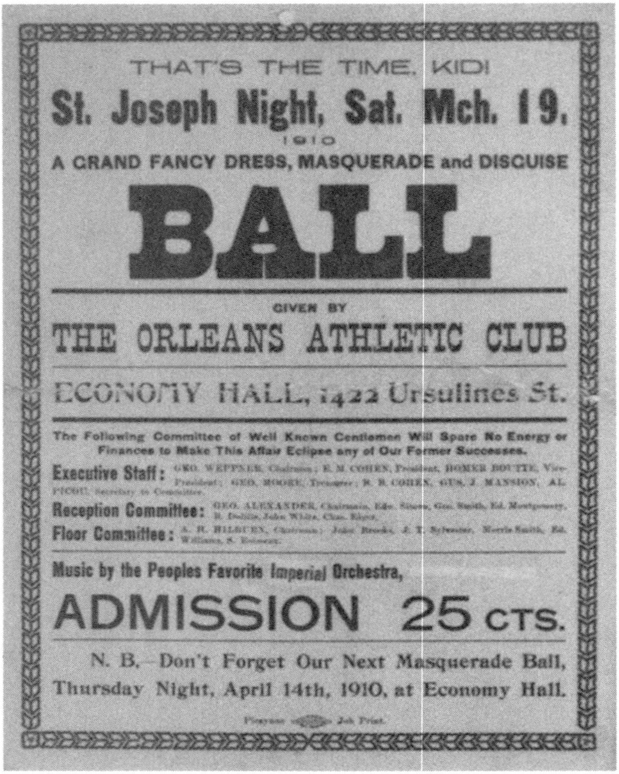

Advertisement for a St. Joseph's Night ball on March 19, 1910. William Russell Jazz Collection, The Historic New Orleans Collection, MSS 520.1005.

Meanwhile, the Sicilians marked the feast of San Giuseppe with a parade through the Fourth and Sixth Districts, followed by a banquet and ball at Majestic Hall. Only one event featured masks: the Epicurean Social Club stuck to tradition with a "fancy dress, masquerade, and calico ball" at Portuguese Hall.[88]

In 1910, Economy Hall, which was known in the mid-1800s for its popular St. Joseph's Day balls for people of color, no longer hosted its own ball but instead held masquerade balls for other groups, such as the Orleans Athletic Club.[89]

In 1911, one of the few remaining St. Joseph's Day events was the Crescent City Carnival Club's fancy dress and masquerade ball, which "commenced at 7:30 with a grand march until midnight." However, these events were no longer all-night affairs "on account of Lenten restrictions."[90] Another indication that St. Joseph's Day as mid-Lent was being forgotten appeared in an article in the *Times-Picayune* headlined "Few Marriage Licenses for St. Joseph's Day": it explained that in "violation of a long established custom there were but seven marriage licenses issued at the City Board of Health yesterday. Inasmuch as to-day is St. Joseph's Day." The clerk noted that the number issued was typically at least three times higher but could offer no explanation for the sharp decrease.[91]

Around this time, descriptions of St. Joseph's Day in New Orleans began to include mentions of Sicilian altars, yet in 1912, there were still some noteworthy dances and balls. One group boasted more than three thousand dancers at the Moose Ball, and another group, the Phoenix Athletic Club, had the only masquerade dance listed, with guests "garbed in the sober regalia of the Ku Klux Clan [*sic*], while others impersonated Spanish senoritas, Grecian ladies, and almost every conceivable disguise. Two gentlemen maskers disguised as Chinamen made the hit of the evening." The article continued, "Good Catholics of this city had a brief respite from the rigors of Lent yesterday and in commemoration of the day of the earthly father of Christ spent St. Joseph's Day attending high masses, feasting, dancing and making merry in a hundred different ways. . . . A feature of the morning ceremonies was a wedding, which is one of the first which has occurred in the church (St. Anthony's Church) during Lent in many years."[92]

That same year, the *New Orleans Item* published a letter from Father Francis Badeaux, coincidentally the first pastor of St. Joseph Parish, who took grave issue with a similar description of how "good Catholics" celebrated St. Joseph's Day:

> I notice on the first page of yesterday's Item an article to the effect that for the space of 24 hours Catholic New Orleans will throw aside the rigors of the Lenten season and that the many restrictions which the church places

upon those who follow this faith will be for the time lifted. The occasion referred to is the feast of St. Joseph, March 19. I believe your reporter is misinformed and his article is misleading.

To use his own words: "The day is usually marked by balls, entertainments and numerous other amusements prior to the advent of more stringent days of the Lenten season," meaning holy week.

As a Catholic priest I have never learned that the church makes an exception to the rules for the Lenten season, either in its general or local regulations. These latter regulations are read in all the churches of the archdiocese on the Sunday preceding Ash Wednesday. They do not except from obligation of fasting on St. Joseph's Day, and they command those who are of state of health does not allow them to fast, to abstain from profane amusements during the whole of Lent.

Your reporter also states that St. Joseph's Day is marked by the celebration of marriages in nearly every church in New Orleans. While marriages may be celebrated quietly in any Catholic church during Lent, the church does not encourage people to marry at this time, and forbids any attendant pomp or display or a nuptial mass.

Kindly publish this letter to correct the wrong impression that your article may produce as to the attitude of the church towards Lenten amusements and marriages.

YOURS TRULY,
Francis Badeaux[93]

Another criticism of celebrating St. Joseph's Day as mid-Lent appeared a year later: "St. Joseph's Day, while not recognized by the Catholic Church as one of intermission in the Lenten penances, is used by some young people for dancing and other forms of entertainment." The attention likely stemmed from the timing of St. Joseph's Day that year because "it comes this year during Holy Week, which all Catholics respect, probably will result in a purely religious observance of the day."[94]

Many residents must have disregarded these critiques: in fact, the *Times-Picayune* proclaimed that St. Joseph's Night was the "one night during the Lenten season when feasting, dancing, and merry making are permissible." These celebrations were not the grand spectacles of old but were mostly parties or smaller gatherings.[95] Yet, on March 17, 1919, the Audubon Lodge No. 182 of the Benevolent Knights of America chartered the steamer *Sidney* for "a grand St. Patrick's masquerade ball for their members and friends," marking the only time masking and the holiday of the Irish were combined. Two days later, the same boat had a "dancing excursion" on St. Joseph's Night, which is "the one big social night of the lenten season."[96]

The Mardi Gras Mystery, written by H. Bedford-Jones and published in 1921, suggested that mid-Lent was nearly forgotten by then:

> What is this Mi-Carême I have been reading about in the papers, anyhow? I thought everything was tight as a clam down here after Mardi Gras! It's still the Lenten season, isn't it? Mardi Gras doesn't come more than once a year, does it?' The secretary smiled. 'Certainly, sir, it's still Lent. But the French people have what they call Mi-Carême or Mid-Lent, and they certainly give it a big celebration! It's a night halfway through Lent, when they can enjoy themselves to the limit—let off steam, as it were.[97]

By the late 1920s, traditional masquerade balls had largely been replaced by the St. Joseph's Day altars of Sicilians and their descendants. Nevertheless, select venues such as the Eagles' Home continued to commemorate mid-Lent with masquerade events, maintaining a vestige of the earlier customs.[98]

Meanwhile, the "Americanized" version of Mardi Gras became the main event and grew into a huge money-maker for New Orleans, drawing both locals and tourists. As Eberhard Faber noted, what happened in New Orleans was "a transformation not imposed from the outside but negotiated, contentiously, by various competing groups of New Orleanians, by American arrivistes and new arrivals from across the Atlantic."[99]

Mardi Gras "happens once in a white man's business-land and again in black-town, once in the brightly lit central city and meanwhile also in the neighborhoods."[100] Initially, St. Joseph's Day celebrations followed suit. However, the original traditions of St. Joseph's Day were kept alive in predominantly Black neighborhoods. Over time, many St. Joseph's Day customs evolved from simple community events into powerful acts of resistance for residents facing ongoing repression in the inner city, helping ensure the survival of these unique customs.

5

BLACK ST. JOSEPH'S NIGHT

The Keepers of the Flame Preserve Masking

On St. Joseph's Night, Mardi Gras Indians chanted and danced their way through the ancestral neighborhoods.

—KEITH WELDON MEDLEY, *Black Life in Old New Orleans*

This [St. Joseph's Night] is the night that is usually a second Mardi Gras for many people.

—ROBERT McKINNEY

When I was big enough to know they had Indians, they had Indians out on St. Joseph's Night.

—BIG CHIEF ROBBE

Marie Laveau, the Voodoo Queen of New Orleans, lived in a small cottage behind a wooden fence on St. Ann Street between Burgundy and North Rampart. Young children played in the yard among the banana trees. Inside the front door, there allegedly stood a beautiful altar and "a large statue of St. Joseph in another corner."[1] A Catholic and Voodoo practitioner, Marie Laveau, sought spiritual guidance from St. Joseph.

The cultural openness in New Orleans fostered and maintained many Afrocentric influences. It also encouraged the development of the syncretic religion Voodoo, which combines elements of European Catholicism with

West African traditions. Zora Neale Hurston remarked that Voodoo "burns with a flame in America, with all the intensity of a suppressed religion." She also observed that Voodoo resembles Christianity in its ability to adapt to its environment.[2] New Orleans, regarded as a "hybrid city," created a space where Africanness could be expressed, but only as a version of Catholicism that dictated social norms. Voodoo thrived in New Orleans because it was shaped to align with Western ideals, rather than its authentic African foundations. "African culture could exist as long as it stayed within the Catholic boundaries," and Catholic St. Joseph found his place in Voodoo practices.[3] St. Joseph is syncretized with Papa Loko, a Voodoo "lwa," or "mysterie," who works with God to help initiate new Voodoo priests and priestesses. He is the first Voodoo priest, the power behind the healing plants and sacred trees, and guardian of the "house." Beyond Voodoo, Black New Orleanians used these adaptations to form a distinctive culture, including the Black Masking Indians on St. Joseph's Night.

"Injuns, here they come!" is the rallying cry on St. Joseph's Night in New Orleans today as the Black Masking Indians take over the evening, emerging from the worn streets in all their feathered glory. These men and women dedicate countless hours to sewing and beading magnificent interpretations of the ceremonial attire of Indigenous peoples. Today, many participants come from diverse backgrounds. However, these "tribes" or "gangs" were initially formed by working-class Black men seeking to elevate their status by paying tribute to another marginalized group: Native Americans. The Black Masking Indians are the only remaining maskers on St. Joseph's Day as mid-Lent.

The Black Masking Indians embody New Orleans's unique hybrid culture that has "remodeled" European and African traditions.[4] Melville Herskovits notes that New Orleans's culture has preserved "more numerous and more specific African practices than in any other portion of the country excepting the Sea Islands." Given the residents' background as Catholic and French, "those aspects of African tradition peculiar to this specialized region have reached their greatest development."[5]

Despite the oppression faced by people of color, the Black Masking Indians preserved their culture, and "culture-contact" not only helped retain

Indians of Yellow Pocahontas at the residence of Chief Paul Joseph in New Orleans, Mardi Gras 1942. WPA Papers, State Library of Louisiana, Wp003427.

it but also led to its reinterpretation and the development of a new cultural identity. Reid Mitchell later described the rise of the Black Masking Indians as "African American sensibility integrating American elements into African traditions and creating a new cultural form." Mardi Gras and St. Joseph's Day helped preserve these traditions and enabled them to thrive.

As early as 1900, Henry Rightor in his *Standard History of New Orleans, Louisiana* referred to Black Masking Indians as part of the "old Carnival"—a Latin institution before Anglo-American modifications—and the krewe of Comus as the "new Carnival," an organized celebration. He believed that "it is the Negroes who preserve in its truest essence the primitive spirit of the Carnival" and of St. Joseph's Day: both days found those Indians "in bands of from six to twenty and upwards, whooping, leaping, brandishing their weapons, and anon, stopping in the middle of the street to go through the movements of a mimic war-dance, chanting while in rhythmic cadence an outlandish jargon of no sensible import to save themselves."[6]

In many formerly colonized countries, enslaved populations controlled various holidays such as Mardi Gras and mid-Lent. However, as the white elite appropriated commercialized celebrations like Mardi Gras in New Orleans, Black traditions continued to thrive within their communities. "Carnival in New Orleans . . . dramatizes the segregation of people, or better, confirms in the festival a separation to which the daily world testifies but the ideological creed categorically denies." Anglo-Americans established hierarchies within Mardi Gras with the development of exclusive krewes and clubs, creating an undercurrent of superiority.[7] On the edges of town, Black residents embraced masking along with "indigenous Carnival customs of grassroots streets celebrations" as seen on Mardi Gras and St. Joseph's Day.[8]

It is difficult to trace the history of Black Masking Indians because of their secrecy and the mainstream press's neglect over the years. What we do know is that like many groups that celebrated St. Joseph's Day with masked balls, the Black Masking Indians also focused on aid and spiritual concerns. However, "unlike second-line clubs the Mardi Gras Indians are not a mass movement but rather a semi-underground phenomenon and the public displays that they are now known for played a subsidiary role in earlier years and the primary motive for the formation of these associations was to provide financial aid to their members."[9] Adding to their secrecy, the Indians initially paraded without permits. They had no established routes nor lists of members, preserving the "old" Carnival attitude of rebellion and tradition, which makes it difficult to know when and where they first appeared.

Indigenous people were present in and around New Orleans throughout the eighteenth and much of the nineteenth centuries. Visitors frequently remarked on the presence of various tribespeople. In 1834, Tyrone Power referred to a group seen at the Place d'Armes "where the Indians usually congregate"; he noted that the "costume of all these people, when divested of the eternal filthy blanket, is showy and at times even becoming and pleasing; bright colors, fringes, tags, beads, and feathers of the ostrich, parroquet, and eagle, constitute the raw material." In his visit to a Choctaw camp in the Bayou St. John area, in one hut "sat the chief and his squaw, upon whose lap lay numberless strings of blue and white beads, which she was admiring and arranging."[10]

One origin story for the Black Masking Indians involves Buffalo Bill's Wild West Show, which visited New Orleans in 1884. It spent four months in winter at Oakland Park, a racetrack now part of the Metairie Country Club; its residency began on December 23 with a parade. In January, a meeting between the enemy chiefs of the Sioux and the Pawnee Tribes led to powwows with Great Plains Indians donning feathered headdresses.[11] Although Black Masking Indians had been masking for years, many believe that the Wild West Show performances instigated changes that increased the number of tribes and the complexity of their physical headdresses. By adopting the style of the performers, their already flamboyant "suits" became even more elaborate. Masking Indians refer to their garb as "suits," likely derived from the French word "*costume*" and the Kreyol word "*kostim,*" both of which translate to English as "suits."

Alternative histories emphasize the significance of Black Hawk in the formation of the Black Masking Indians. The Sauk warrior from a Midwestern Native American tribe was captured and taken on a tour to share his story. Although he died in 1838, Black Hawk became an essential part of New Orleans's history—but not until the arrival of Leafy Anderson, who established the first Black Spiritual church in New Orleans around 1918.[12] However, a reference appears in *Southern Travels,* published in 1834, about a "Museum Boat—a floating collection of curiosities" in St. Louis, which included Black Hawk, the "Prophet." "Black Hawk addressed the company . . . he was now very poor" and would perform a war dance for "a collection of ten to fifteen dollars."[13] Conceivably, Black Hawk could have stopped in New Orleans, or perhaps New Orleans's river workers could have shared information about the great Native American.

Another mention of men dressed as Indians was found in a small book of recollections from the 1880s on Mardi Gras Day:

At about 10:00 a.m. that day there was a band of men (about 60) disguised as Indians who wore real Indian costumes and their chiefs had turkey feathers running down from around their heads way down in the back. They came along from St. Bernard Avenue on Robertson Street, shouting and screaming war whoops and carried tomahawks–on their way would stop and perform war dances, etc., and would run for a block and begin again. Though we were frightened when very young we always waited for the passing of the "Indians."[14]

George Washington Cable's book *The Grandissimes,* published in 1880 but set in 1804, depicts a scene at Congo Square where "the blackest of black man, an athlete of superb figure, in breeches of 'Indienne'—the stuff used for slave women's best dresses—jingling with bells, his feet in moccasins, his tight crisp hair decked out with feathers, a necklace of alligator's teeth rattling on his breast and a living serpent twined about his neck."[15]

It would not be unreasonable to say that, through daily contact, Black New Orleanians would begin to imitate Indigenous people and gather the necessary items to create a "suit." Traditionally, the days and nights of those who mask Indian are spent building, beading, and feathering their stunning wearable art pieces to be worn for two days—Mardi Gras and St. Joseph's Day—before they are destroyed or dismantled. Under the influence of their "suits," these men and women are transformed into warriors, chiefs, and queens, chanting with powerful, gratitude-filled voices that echo through their neighborhoods. It remains a great honor to carry on the legacy of this local neighborhood tradition.

"Many are called, but few are chosen," Big Chief Darryl Montana, son of Big Chief Allison "Tootie" Montana of the Yellow Pocahontas, says of the Masking Indians: "You can like it, but you have to love it until the day you die. Being a Big Chief is the most incredible privilege of all. The Big Chief of an Indian gang requires the skills of an army general and the responsibility of a concerned parent."[16] It is not as simple as merely crafting a "suit" and showing up; it is a game of chess with strategies in place where rituals are enacted following a set hierarchy; much of the rivalry between

Black Masking Indians in New Orleans in the 1930s.
WPA Papers, State Library of Louisiana, Wp003425.

tribes reflect the strife in much of the city—downtown vs. uptown based on a "warrior culture."[17] According to Charles Siler, "tradition went from one of violence to one where beauty became the standard."[18] The Indians today win battles not by physically fighting but by creating the prettiest "suit."

This celebration of Native Americans in New Orleans's Black society connected their community to "courage, defiance, and independence." It established St. Joseph's Night as a time of respite during Lent and of honoring ancestors and the spirit of rebellion they saw in the Indigenous people of America. The meetings of the tribes represent and "commemorate the dramatic contact between Africans and other exploited people of the New World colonies—the Native Americans."[19] Because costuming was acceptable on Mardi Gras and St. Joseph's Day, the Black Masking Indians' dancing evoked less resistance and negative attention. Initially, according to Royce Osborn, masking as Indians "gave enslaved Africans the illusion of freedom and allowed free people of color to escape the bonds of a segregated society through fantasy and performance," but under the protection of a masking holiday.[20] Big Chief Robbe confirmed in Al Kennedy's book, *Chief of Chiefs,* that he masked in homage to the Native Americans who had lived in the area and hid and protected runaway slaves. He said, "If a slave made it to the Indians, there wasn't a master going to look for him there."[21]

Jeroen Dewulf connects old procession traditions to Laetare Sunday, the fourth Sunday of Lent. This day, which is akin to mid-Lent, represents a break and a moment of joy in the season of austerity: it is sanctioned by the Catholic Church and associated with a parade of lanterns. Lanterns also played a significant role in early Indian celebrations on St. Joseph's Night. Big Chief Robbe recalls that the Indians were permitted to mask in the streets until midnight, provided they carried lanterns to avoid frightening residents. He explained that the kerosene lamps used by the Sewerage and Water Board of New Orleans were frequently "borrowed" by the Indians that night as a means of complying with the law. These lamps were ready to illuminate the night after receiving a fresh coat of paint. Black New Orleanians also lit the way for the white Carnival clubs as "the chief torchbearers in the nocturnal processions; and it is they who, clothed in *bizarre* gaberdines made of glazed calico in various hues, have led the interminable trains of mules which dragged the 'floats' or wains on which the glittering pageants were displayed."[22] Today, Black men still lead some white Krewes with flaming torches known as "flambeaux."

Kinser points out, "The Mardi Gras Indians developed a Carnival freedom toward *ritual* independence of the white society by which they were dominated every day but this one, devoted to pure fantasy. They developed confrontational rituals which, for all their merriment, had a severe side and expressed in aggressive and artistic ways the cohesion of neighbors."[23] Kinser invokes Mardi Gras Day, but perhaps St. Joseph's Night has become more significant after most of the city abandoned mid-Lent costuming. This night belongs to the Indians, allowing them to march without the distractions of other celebrants, as is the case on Mardi Gras. Their "*ritual* independence of white society" becomes apparent when St. Joseph's Day is overlooked by white society, leaving the Indians to take center stage one night each year.

Because Mardi Gras and St. Joseph's Day were traditional masking days in New Orleans, they created a safe space for residents, particularly people of color, to engage in acts of subversion disguised as celebrations for fellow people of color. As early as 1781, Black New Orleanians were prohibited from masking or even wearing feathers.[24] Such rules were resented in a city where, as George Sala noted during his 1880 visit, there was "an abundance of black faces," unlike other coastal towns in the United States. The New Orleans Black community was "seen," but they challenged their position in society through masking.

As a travel writer, Sala had visited other cities during Carnival—Paris, Brussels, Cologne, Milan, Venice, Rome, Turin, and Nice—and concluded that New Orleans possessed a "thoroughly new, original, and weirdly picturesque element" that he had not encountered before. He attributed this unique quality to the Black residents "masquerading on their own private account. They have been capering about the streets arrayed in the most absurd dresses, and cutting the most ridiculous capers." They donned various costumes on Canal Street, including "Uncle Toms."[25] The rise of white carnival krewes magnified the exclusion of Black New Orleanians, leading to the emergence of Black traditions throughout the city.[26]

Although not often featured in travel brochures, Black Carnival krewes, including Zulu emerged in the late nineteenth and early twentieth centuries. Even though early festivities were enjoyed by all, the concept of "authenticity" in Mardi Gras soon became closely tied to white culture; this left little space for public displays by Black New Orleanians to celebrate outside their neighborhoods.[27] By most accounts, these public displays were limited to Carnival time: black krewes appeared but did not parade on St. Joseph's Day.

A dancing and singing group on a New Orleans street in the 1930s.
WPA Papers, State Library of Louisiana, Wp002867.

However, in their neighborhoods, "Negroes celebrate St. Joseph's Night by donning their Mardi Gras costumes, a particular custom dating back many years. On South Rampart Street, blacks, browns and high yellows step high, wide and fancy, and there are numerous balls and dances," thereby connecting the day to mid-Lent. The holiday remained significant in New Orleans's Black community at the dawn of the 1940s. Indeed, Zulu, the foremost Black Carnival krewe, held a dance on St. Joseph's Day at its then-headquarters on South Rampart Street "as its first entertainment to raise funds for the 1942 Carnival parade."[28] Robert McKinney reiterates that "March 19, always an important date in the New Orleans calendar, has been a second Mardi Gras to Negroes for the past two decades. It is tradition that Zulus, Indians and Baby Dolls don their costumes that night and revive the spirit of Fat Tuesday for a few hours. There are no parades, of course, but they wander about on foot, visiting bars, having dances and parties at various places, strutting their stuff."[29]

Anthony Jeanjacques, born in 1935 and raised in the Tremé neighborhood, remembered that St. Joseph's Day was as significant as Mardi Gras. He noted that everyone in his neighborhood dressed in costumes and celebrated in the streets. He also recalled seeing not only the Black Masking Indians but also the Baby Dolls, who dressed up for the occasion, confirming that the festivities in Tremé remained vibrant until the 1940s.[30]

The Baby Dolls, a female group whose members dress up as dolls, are traditionally recognized for their costumes on Mardi Gras. Photographs and interviews from the 1930s and 1940s indicate that they also dressed up for St. Joseph's Day, although this tradition was likely discontinued shortly thereafter. In 2007, Keith Weldon Medley interviewed Miss Esther Barnum Green, a longtime resident of the Tremé, about life in the old neighborhood. Born in 1928, Miss Esther vividly recalls Carnival Day, explicitly mentioning the annual visit from the "Baby Dolls." She also noted that the Mardi Gras Indians passed her house not only on Carnival Day but also on St. Joseph's Night.[31] Her recollections suggest that the association of the Baby Dolls with St. Joseph's Day had diminished or ceased by the late 1940s.

According to Beatrice Hill, who claimed to be the first Baby Doll, the group of female sex workers first paraded in 1912 on Mardi Gras after gathering to discuss how they would costume that year. She recalled, "A gal named Althea Brown jumps up and says, 'Let's be ourselves. Let's be Baby Dolls; that's what the pimps always calls us." The Million-Dollar Baby Dolls were born that day, and the tradition of masking as Baby Dolls began.[32] Robert McKinney noted that "the Million Dollar Baby Dolls were among those who celebrated on St. Joseph's night. This is the night that is a second Mardi Gras for a lot of people, i.e. the Baby Dolls and their ilk. They mask and wave their hips, sing low down blues Songs to the accompaniment of loud cornets, banjos, drums and other instruments. They frolic on the streets in the same manner as they do on Fat Tuesday; their shimmies are strictly 'solid' and always attract a large crowd."[33]

The Baby Dolls appeared "as innocent as possible, which may be accepted as a perfect example of altering one's personality," wearing skirts and bloomers of "chaste pink or virginal blue, the skirts pleated, the bloomers trimmed with ruffles and little bows. They wear waists or halters to match and bonnets that tie demurely beneath their chins. Their dusky faces, framed by long corkscrew curls of every shade, are heavily rouged and powdered. Some wear pink and blue socks, but most prefer long hose held up on their dark thighs with flashy, ruffled garters."[34] These women dressed as dolls but danced, acted provocatively, and fought.

Beatrice Hill was a darker-skinned woman who lived uptown, not downtown near the lighter-skinned Creoles. By singing and "walkin' raddy," smoking cigars, and acting in ways acceptable only to men while dressed so innocently, she and her fellow Baby Dolls reclaimed their power.[35] However, there were deeper reasons behind their costuming and parading. These uptown Baby Dolls sought to "tease and irritate their rivals" downtown, thereby emphasizing the rivalry between uptown and downtown, as well as the distinction between Creole and non-Creole.

A Baby Doll celebration in New Orleans in 1942. These dancers are likely the Gold Diggers, with their cohorts dressed in gold satin on St. Joseph's Night. WPA Papers, State Library of Louisiana, Wp002956.

Baby Doll celebration, 1942, part of Mardi Gras in New Orleans, La. These men are likely affiliated with the Gold Diggers Social Aid and Pleasure Club, and it is probably St. Joseph's Day. WPA Papers, State Library of Louisiana, Wp002947.

Later, another group similar to the Baby Dolls appeared on St. Joseph's Night, fueling a new rivalry. The Gold Diggers Social Aid and Pleasure Club in 1936 "dressed somewhat like baby dolls, but their costumes were of yellow gold satin" with matching shoes. They typically had men accompanying them who were dressed "also in gold, light yellow trousers, white shirts and 'blouses,' and black shoes." By 1940, the Gold Diggers had fifteen members, and they paraded together, along with a man "masked as a policeman."[36]

An obscure 1951 pamphlet, filled with recollections of the Robertson Street area in the 1880s, mentioned a group of ladies parading on Mardi Gras Day. St. Joseph's Day was not included in the short list of parading holidays, which is not surprising given the publication date. The author, Elise Kirsch, did recall her childhood fear of the Black Masking Indians and continued with this story:

> There were bands of women who also had Domino costumes, some in colored percale, others in curtain material and some with lace curtains draped on their shoulders—they wore these costumes over two or more voluminous petticoats; some of these belonged to the people for whom they washed and they were elaborately trimmed with lace and embroidery—they usually carried a latanier[37] fan and wielded it constantly—they also wore the horse-hair mask. When they met a man that any of their crowd knew he was a "goner" for they would wheel him around one after the other until he was dazed (these were mostly colored people), but they made things lively on our street. Though Claiborne Street was their avenue on that day.[38]

The women described might have been an earlier version of the Baby Dolls or a group that later influenced them. They were bold women who, disguised by masking, took to the streets feeling free enough to grab at men during the two days designated to challenge social norms. Perhaps they aimed to create a celebration similar to that of the washerwomen parade in Paris on mid-Lent, where the lowly ladies of laundering became queens for a day. In the 1960s and 1970s, a few groups of Baby Dolls were still strutting their stuff in Black neighborhoods during Mardi Gras, but by this time, St. Joseph's Night was exclusively reserved for the Indians.

One elusive group that vanished yet left their mark on St. Joseph's Night was the Western Girls, a collective of Black "female impersonators" who dressed as Annie Oakley one year, revealing the origin of their name. Led by a vibrant character who called herself Corinne the Queen, they proudly showcased their queer sexuality and were arguably the wildest group to participate in both Mardi Gras Day and St. Joseph's Night.

The flamboyant Western Girls were in their glory on that night. "In evening gowns and wigs, they try to outdo the real girls. The ones who top their extremely dark faces with golden-blonde and flaming red wigs are the funniest." Corinne always maintained her regal bearing, explaining, "I'm a real queen, and don't nobody forget it!" Corinne the Queen even claimed to have been Queen Zulu in 1931.[39] Marcus Christian's unpublished book "The

Negro in Louisiana" reveals that from 1923 to 1933, male Zulu queens were the norm. Later, cis-women reigned as queens.[40] Further research confirms that Corinne served as the Queen of Zulu in 1931, 1933, and possibly 1932, alongside King Zulu Allen Leon for two of those years.[41]

The 1940s brought several changes to St. Joseph's Day that may have contributed to a significant decline in its festivities. In 1940, masking was banned because St. Joseph's Day fell within Holy Week, the week leading up to Easter Sunday, one of the most important times in the Catholic calendar. Archbishop Joseph Francis Rummel, a German with little appreciation for Mardi Gras and probably even less for St. Joseph's Day, chose to prohibit masking and celebrations. Robert McKinney reported, "The archbishop stepped into the picture and said that there should not be any masking because it fell in the Lenten Season. He suggested April 2 instead." The captain of the First Precinct made sure that the residents in the precinct's neighborhoods knew that he would arrest anyone who "masked" that day.[42]

One of the Baby Dolls, Jenny Watts, asked why the archbishop could tell them what to do; none of her fellow Baby Dolls could answer her because they did not know of his power within the church nor why they should care what he said. The original Baby Dolls lived and worked uptown, so they might not have been Catholic and were probably not Creoles. Most of them initially ignored his threat and promised to wear masks. According to one Baby Doll, Captain Jackson personally contacted them and threatened them with jail time when he learned of their intentions. Many of the Baby Dolls took the threat seriously and chose not to mask, including "Baby" Irene, who opted to stay home because she had just been released from jail and had no plans to return there. One of the few Baby Dolls to mask mentioned that she only did so because a journalist and photographer from the Federal Writers' Project had contacted her. She referred to her Baby Doll costume as her "suit," a term that today is synonymous with Black Masking Indian costumes. This reinforces the idea that the term likely originated as a translation of the French word "costume" or the Kreyol word "kostim," which means "suit" in English. Although a large crowd gathered to see the Baby Dolls, only three appeared in costume, the fewest in more than twenty years. "One of the more peppery Baby Dolls said she didn't give a damn what the Archbishop said she was going to mask, and she did so."[43]

Later that same night, a few Black Masking Indians appeared unmasked, having taken the threat more seriously than the Baby Dolls. They sang their songs, played tambourines, and engaged in some "rather mild" dancing. However, as the night wore on, a few more Indians showed up, including one who was dressed in "white with red trimmings and blue lines, beads hung from his neck, and feathers drooped from his side. He was a spy boy, handling a lantern and an extra wide crown of assorted feathers." Rumors spread through the streets that an Indian ball was starting at the Japanese Tea Room. About twelve Indians arrived to dance and sing their traditional songs. Still, the expected crowd failed to show up because, as one onlooker said, "You kin never tell about them Indians. They might come this way, but they change their mind. They don't know where they gonna sometimes go."[44]

Unlike past St. Joseph's Day celebrations, the night was tame. When asked about Captain Jackson's threat of arrest, the chief of the Indian tribe replied that he did not know who he was and that his tribe had planned on masking on both March 19 and April 2. One of the unmasked Indians observed that "whoever it was who changed [the date of] St. Joseph Night is got some power cause the people aint out like they used to be."[45] Nevertheless, many people masked on St. Joseph's Night and celebrated boldly on both days.

In 1940, the local police enforced not a civil law but a decision by the Catholic archdiocese to change the date of celebration. This showed that the Catholic Church still exerted some control over the city. Meanwhile, the local newspaper advertised that a "St. Joseph Night masquerade will be celebrated aboard the *Steamer Capitol,*" complete with dancing, music, and "fun-making."[46] Perhaps the boat was exempt from the order because it was on the water, beyond the reach of Archbishop Rummel and Captain Jackson of the New Orleans Police Department.

Some Black clubs seized the opportunity to host parties on both days. The Tick Tock Tavern on South Rampart Street held a "Masquerade and

Baby Doll celebration, March 19, 1942. Written on photo:
"Unmasked Indians 'breaking down' with a gypsy woman at Pete's Blue Heaven."
WPA Papers, State Library of Louisiana, Wp002945.

Disguise Ball" on St. Joseph's Night, Tuesday, March 19, and a "Big Masquerade Ball Celebrating St. Joseph's Night" on Tuesday, April 2. Admission for the second St. Joseph's Night was higher because it featured the "Carolina Cotton Pickers 15-piece orchestra," touted as "America's Newest Orchestra Sensation!"[47] Meanwhile, the Gypsy Tea Room, located at St. Ann and South Villere streets, another popular spot for the Indians and Baby Dolls, held only one "Grand Masquerade Dance" on Tuesday, March 19, 1940, the actual St. Joseph's Night.[48]

A few years later, the country was at war, and Chief Robbe could not recall seeing any Indians in the streets during wartime. He observed that their "Mardi Gras spending for fun" had evolved into "the patriotic buying of defense bonds and stamps."[49] Spending on St. Joseph's Night celebrations similarly decreased great. The year after World War II ended, 1946, the Indians emerged as possibly the only group celebrating St. Joseph's Night.

In 1946, the Robin Hood Club, located in an uptown neighborhood, hosted a "St. Joseph Nite Dance" featuring Clyde Kerr Sr. and his orchestra.[50] In 1999, his son Clyde Kerr Jr. reflected on another performance held on St. Joseph's Night, this time at the ILA Auditorium at 2700 South Claiborne Avenue, where he had the privilege of judging the best Indian "suit." Big Chief Donald Harrison recalled a specific event on St. Joseph's Night in 1949 at the Lincoln Theater on Freret Street and Washington Avenue. This theater, designed for people of color, accommodated 1,500 individuals. The stage was so spacious that at least one hundred Indians could fit on it at the same time. Each "tribe" performed a song and displayed their "suits." Big Chief Robbe noted that after all the performances, the theater owner would come onto the stage and declare the winner, based on the level of the applause received. The winner would receive either ten dollars or supplies for their next suit. Edwin Harrison, the brother of Big Chief Donald Harrison, shared that the "St. Joseph's Night competitions for the prettiest Indian" were held at the Municipal Auditorium and featured national artists like B.B. King. He declared, "We had just as much fun on St. Joseph's Night as Carnival Day."

According to Donald Harrison, these competitions began as gatherings in the streets but later were held in theaters in various neighborhoods. Indian tribes would meet at the theater after parading through their communities and "whoever wanted to participate . . . had a certain time if they wanted to be judged."[51] They may have moved indoors in response to the date change in 1940: when asked if she was worried about being arrested that night, one of the Baby Dolls answered, "There is always an inside."[52] Being indoors enabled Black residents to avoid scrutiny and hostility after the rest of the city had forgotten the masking aspect of St. Joseph's Day.

In 1990 Super Sunday, held in March each year, was created to provide another opportunity for the Indians to parade. It also introduced a commercial element. Big Chief Donald Harrison of the Guardians of the

Flame Indians spoke of the "commercial thing," where Black Masking Indians were invited to don their suits for payment. This differed from the "natural thing" Chief Harrison described as "a wonderful and natural tradition for the Mardi Gras Indians to make their appearances on Mardi Gras Day and St. Joseph's Night."[53]

The history of Black Masking Indians is filled with stories of warring "tribes," often leading to physical confrontations among masked Indians. Historically, tribes resembled gangs in many cities; they represented specific neighborhoods and were frequently composed of members from the same family, who paraded together to protect the names and reputations of all their "tribe." Big Chief Donald Harrison believed that the decrease in Indian battles during the 1940s was due to many men being tired of violence and just wanting to enjoy themselves after serving in the war. This made it safer for all New Orleanians to view the Indians. Finding the Black Masking Indians on Mardi Gras and St. Joseph's Day became increasingly popular among New Orleanians and visitors as they no longer feared incidents of violence.

Interestingly, the increase in the size and weight of their suits was directly related to the decline in violence and the rise of tourism in New Orleans. Over the years, they evolved from easily manageable costumes to enormous works of art. The "emphasis on the headpiece correlates with the decline of violence and the rise of tourism in New Orleans. This huge and unwieldy costume immobilizes the chief," so he was unable to fight or attack a neighboring tribe.[54]

Throughout the years, many historians, documentarians, and the media regarded Black celebrations as less significant than those of white New Orleanians, aligning with the older idea that "'authentic' Mardi Gras was a white celebration, and blacks were to be segregated and excluded from public space."[55] Police harassment often troubled the Indians, particularly on St. Joseph's Night. Yet one incident showed that some still relished the spectacle of this "old Carnival." Chief Robbe and several of his Indians were arrested one St. Joseph's Night for disturbing the peace. During their appearance at night court, the judge lashed out at the arresting officer and asked,

A masked Indian with three people dressed in clown costumes.
Photo by Fonville Winans, reproduced courtesy of the Winans family.

"Where do you come from? You can't be coming from New Orleans!" He continued, "These boys have been out from six to twelve on St. Joseph when I was in short pants," and he released them.[56]

Indeed, Big Chief Robbe recalled that his "tribe" sang their songs and met with other "tribes" on the streets of New Orleans from six o'clock until midnight on St. Joseph's Night. Before heading out, he remembered enjoying meals at the Italian grocery stores in the neighborhood on St. Joseph's Day, where he visited their altars. Perhaps the Sicilian meal and camaraderie soothed the Indians—Robbe noted on St. Joseph's Night, "They didn't holler and carry on like they did on Carnival Day."[57] Later, Big Chief Donald Harrison also recalled that these Sicilian-owned "corner stores" had "stops" that provided the Indians a place to get food and rest on St. Joseph's Night.

Bernard Walter Lomax, who first masked in 1949, wrote a song in 1950 called "Shallow Water," which Indians sing to this day. He claimed that the chorus is "taken from an Italian song."[58] This song offers another glimpse into the budding relationships between Black New Orleanians and their immigrant neighbors, who lived nearby and owned many businesses in the Black neighborhoods.

New Orleans became New Orleans with its customs and culture, not because of specific French, Spanish, Indigenous, African, or Sicilian influences, but because of the impact of all these cultures in the city. The Black Masking Indians represent a form of cultural assimilation and syncretism in its prettiest form. Thankfully, the Black Masking Indians continue to mask, and their costuming on mid-Lent remains a vital cultural artifact to the community. Without their celebration, the observance of St. Joseph's Day in New Orleans would perhaps have disappeared.

St. Joseph's Night offered Black residents another opportunity after Mardi Gras to "stage their ritual interpretations of history," with the Indian "suits," women's attire, and dressing as a child all serving as "cover for an identity, rebellious and haunting, a body presence of freedom and revolt against the policeman, judge or Rex upon his high throne."[59] Dewulf views this as an opportunity for one part of the New Orleans community to reconnect with its history, even if it is under the guise of a "carnivalesque smokescreen."[60] These gatherings morphed into political speech.[61] Parading in groups, they were both seen and protected, and as a result, they became less vulnerable. By masquerading as Indians, they elevated their status by recreating themselves as regal works of art, simultaneously invoking and subverting stereotypes by disrupting life in the streets and public spaces where marginalized people could gather and express themselves.

Race and repression created a vital space for expression among both Black and Sicilian New Orleanians, with their lives often intertwining. The Black Masking Indians played a key role in preserving the traditions of St. Joseph's Day in New Orleans, helping ensure the survival of its celebrations. Likewise, the mutual influence of neighbors helped protect the Sicilian altars, which fed the Indians both figuratively and literally. These altars are a unique and lasting legacy within the city's cultural fabric.

6

SICILIAN CELEBRATIONS

St. Joseph's Day Is "Altared"

> To the stranger the altars are a conglomeration of paper flowers and statuary, vegetables, fruits, great platters of stuffed artichokes, bread and confections—but to the children of Italy they represent a mystic union of the good things of heaven and earth.
>
> —*Item-Tribune,* March 19, 1933

> The saint that personifies luck to all true believers.
>
> —*Times-Picayune,* March 20, 1917

Arguably, one of the most unusual St. Joseph's Day observances in New Orleans occurred in 1903 at the Orleans Parish Prison. It involved Antonio Luciano, a man of Sicilian heritage, who was accused of murder and involved in one of the most sensational trials the city had ever seen.[1] It all started in May 1902 with an argument at Luciano's store on Poydras Street, located between Saratoga and Rampart Streets. The conflict escalated, culminating a month later in a gunfight outside the old Pilié Market that resulted in two deaths and three injuries. Among the casualties was Salvatore, Antonio's brother. At Salvatore's funeral, pallbearers were noticeably absent because they feared retaliation from associates of the powerful, allegedly mafia-connected Giancona family, who may have instigated the altercation. Meanwhile, at the funeral, Antonio realized that a man who smirked at him after kissing his dead brother's forehead was, in fact, Salvatore's murderer. With that, he dragged the man into the yard and killed him. Antonio was arrested and sent to the Parish Prison to await his trial.[2]

Antonio and his family prayed earnestly to St. Joseph for his acquittal. Before his troubles began, he had proclaimed that "the saint was daily reverenced" because St. Joseph was both his favorite saint and the patron saint of Sicily, where his family originated.

Celebrations of mid-Lent, known as *mezza Quaresima*, or Half-Lent, were part of Sicily's religious life. A centerpiece of these events was the construction of an effigy of an old woman, symbolizing the time of penance; it was cut in half to signal to the citizens that the fasting period was nearly over. Some towns created a puppet representing the old lady, which was cut in half and burned, bringing much joy and celebration.[3]

However, it was not this festival that was transported to Louisiana; it was the feast of St. Joseph. After being found not guilty, Antonio arranged for a high mass to be celebrated at the prison chapel, where he presented two gold crowns to be placed on the statues of the baby Jesus and St. Joseph. He then hosted a St. Joseph's Day feast with spaghetti and wine on long tables in the prison yard. Everyone was welcome to join Luciano's feast, Black and white prisoners alike.

Sicily and New Orleans have been connected since the city's earliest days. Trade between these regions began during the colonial era, with a focus on the citrus import business. By 1850, more southern Italians and Sicilians resided in New Orleans than in any other city in the United States.[4] Many early settlers were skilled workers, ranging from physicians to perfumers. However, most operated food-related businesses, such as coffee houses, grocery stores, importers, liquor stores, and a "vermicelli and chocolate manufacturer."[5]

A second wave of migration occurred after the Civil War ended and following passage of the Thirteenth Amendment. In 1866, the Louisiana Bureau of Sugar Planters created the Louisiana Bureau of Immigration to attract labor to the state's sugar plantations, which urgently needed seasonal workers to replace the previously enslaved workforce. Sicilian peasants, familiar with migrant labor, responded in large numbers to the bureau's recruitment campaigns; most who arrived were peasants, rather than members of the merchant class.[6]

At around the same time, Sicily's economy plummeted. "Conscription, increased unemployment, higher rents and prices and a new kind of stamp tax, all these added to the misery caused by a dry spring and a food shortage, and made trouble almost inevitable." Sicilians in the newly formed Italy were considered the "Southern Problem"; in fact, Italy bombed the city of Palermo for several days after riots broke out, resulting in the Seven and a Half Days Revolt. Once the unrest subsided, the Italians stationed a significant portion of their army there, which only fostered resentment among Sicilians. This military presence encouraged many to leave for seasonal work and potentially improve their lives through higher wages.[7]

As a port town, New Orleans welcomed newcomers from around the world, contributing to its diverse population and fluid racial dynamics; it offered immigrants a sense of agency that was rare in other American cities. Sicilians integrated more quickly than in many other areas of the United States, partly because they found in New Orleans a strongly Catholic community that embraced their religious and cultural practices—in contrast to other large cities like New York or Baltimore, where Protestants initially sought to suppress Catholicism.[8] In New Orleans, they celebrated the same holidays, honored the same saints, and encountered no segregation or relegation to any particular neighborhood. "New Orleans was not merely a physical island; it was also an island of French and Spanish culture in an Anglo-Saxon Sea."[9] However, like any mass migration, the Sicilians encountered significant challenges, facing not only racism but also a form of "ethnicism." They often found solace by settling among another marginalized group: Black New Orleanians.

The largest wave of mass migration started in the 1880s. By 1890, New Orleans's population included about 11,000 Sicilians; by 1910, this number had grown to approximately 24,000. In the early twentieth century, the grand, formally organized mid-Lent balls on St. Joseph's Day were being phased out. However, a different tradition emerged in the streets and homes of Sicilian immigrant families. Altars and processions honoring St. Joseph started to appear throughout the city, particularly in the neighborhoods where Sicilians had settled.

The earliest recorded celebration of St. Joseph's Day in New Orleans that featured Sicilians took place in 1872 during Reconstruction. Tiro al Bersaglio, which means "hit the target," is a militia group that still exists today and is one of the few that is legally recognized (see chapter 4). According to its website, this group was founded in 1868 and was chartered as a "mutual benefit society and marksman club" on March 10, 1869.[10] Established during the early wave of Sicilian immigration to New Orleans, it mostly comprised merchants, unlike the later influx of peasants. The procession in 1872 was held to honor Giuseppe (Joseph) Garibaldi on his name day, corresponding to the feast day of St. Joseph. Tiro al Bersaglio held the procession "on the principal street" for St. Joseph's Day, and the marchers were Italian citizens.[11]

In 1875, the society hosted a "public parade in military uniform," once again, in honor of their countryman Joseph (Giuseppe) Garibaldi. Unfortunately, the company had lost all its muskets the year before, so "the parade will be without arms unless the members succeed in borrowing some for the occasion."[12] On St. Joseph's Day in 1878, a procession with an accompanying supper was held once again in honor of General Giuseppe Garibaldi.[13]

In 1880, while many New Orleanians continued celebrating with masked balls, the Italian community ventured outside the city to host an event at a restaurant near Lake Pontchartrain: "The Tiro Al Bersaglio Capt. S. D'Amico will celebrate St. Joseph's Day in honor of the Italian patriot leader, Joseph Garibaldi, with a parade and dinner at Jno (John) Astredo's restaurant at the New Lake End." In 1881, another "parade and dinner" were held at the same restaurant.[14] Either these celebrations were not held again or were not advertised because the city's tolerance of its Sicilian immigrants had lessened. As more Sicilians flooded the city, attitudes changed because of "a growing concern over Italian and Sicilian economic competition, resentment over their commercial success, and ambivalence regarding their intermingling with the black community."[15]

In addition, newspapers in New Orleans were then filled with stories about Sicilian violence and organized crime, reflecting concerns that Sicilian assimilation into American life was impossible. As early as 1866, the *Daily Picayune* published an article about two Sicilian friends who shared a room and "loved the same piece of calico." This jealousy escalated to a physical, "savage" fight over the girl, stemming from the "traits of the race." Later, Sicilians were often portrayed as criminals or linked to what the *Times-Picayune* referred to as the "one thing mysterious and terrible in the police records of our city over another: the Italian vendetta indulged in by a large portion of the lugger fruit men and others within the 'Dago' population of the city." These negative portrayals increased significantly during the latter part of the nineteenth century.[16]

In 1890, David Hennessy, the police chief of New Orleans, was murdered, and members of the Sicilian community were blamed for the crime. Nineteen men were arrested, but none were convicted, which fueled anger and resentment among white New Orleanians—culminating in the lynching of eleven of the men. Many believed that the acquittals had sparked celebrations among the Sicilians. The non-Sicilian community, in their ignorance, did not realize that the celebrations were merely preparations for the birthday of Italian King Umberto, which was on the day of the lynching, March 14, and for St. Joseph's Day a few days later. Some New Orleanians and Americans across the country reacted angrily, perceiving these celebrations to be an insult to what they believed was a miscarriage of justice.[17] Many felt the lynchings were justified.

Anthony Bennett, the leader of the Original Royal Players Brass Band, recalled a story his grandmother had shared with him about the Hennessy murder. "People were running around the city yelling, 'They killa da chief! They killa da chief!' They started rounding up Sicilians. Her uncle could have easily been mistaken for one of them. They had to hide him in the vegetable cart to sneak him out of the neighborhood. It was hard to distinguish between many Sicilians and Blacks back then."[18] His grandmother lived then in the Tremé, one of the neighborhoods where the new immigrants settled. The Sicilian community suffered greatly after the incident.

A few years later, the infamous "haunted house," the LaLaurie mansion on Royal Street in the French Quarter, was referred to as a "house accursed" by one author in 1895. This label was given not because of the murders committed by the property's former owner but because of the new tenants.[19] "It was a receptacle of the scum of Sicilian immigrants, and the fumes of the malodorous filth which emanated from its interiors." He claimed that the Sicilians had taken over the marketplaces, creating an "offensive species of peddling and 'dago' shops, not only in antagonism to traditional customs, but dangerous to public health."[20]

The aftermath of the Hennessy affair may have instilled fear in the Sicilian community, leading to more subdued festivities or even their cancellation. However, after a few years, the celebrations returned, but in a different form: many events were replete with patriotic rhetoric and actions, possibly aimed at reducing the anger felt by other New Orleanians. This was a pivotal time for Sicilians in New Orleans: they stood on the brink of becoming outcasts or exotic "others." They navigated these threats better than expected.

In 1902, the Italian Mutual Benevolent Association, an Italian organization founded in the 1840s, had its inaugural grand ball at Pythian Hall on St. Joseph's Day. However, this affair was not a masquerade ball.[21] On March 19, 1906, members of the St. Joseph Mutual Benefit Society gathered at a hall "to take part in speeches and the christening of an American flag and of an Italian flag." Afterward, the group marched to St. Alphonsus Church, where they blessed the flags and listened to a "short and patriotic address reminding the Italian residents of their obligations to the country that has given them an opportunity of earning their livelihood in peace and which guarantees them every protection while they continue to obey the laws of the land."[22]

A few years later, Commodore and Mrs. Patorno hosted a social affair in the French Quarter to celebrate the feast of St. Joseph with a reception and dance; the Italian vice consul was one of the guests. The commodore was a civic leader and an important politician. The party at their house in the French Quarter (now the Cornstalk Fence Hotel) was decorated in a "Japanese style," and "cakes and ices of variegated hues were served by young ladies in Japanese costumes," followed by a midnight supper.[23] It was described as "one of the most fashionable receptions held in the lower section of the city in a long while" and was attended by "the most prominent residents of the Italian colony and a few of the American friends of the commodore and his wife."[24] The Creole part of town was no longer considered fashionable, because the Anglo-Americans who resided uptown had taken control of business and social events.

After years of subdued Americanized celebrations, several associations reemerged with a renewed sense of "Italianness" in the early years of the twentieth century. In 1908, Società Italiana di Mutua Beneficio San Giuseppe held two days of festivities, recognized as "one of the best known Italian [note: not Sicilian] societies of the upper section"; perhaps it was promoted as an Italian society to distinguish its members from the more recent immigrants of peasant origin. In addition, the society's name, which had earlier been translated into English, returned to its original Italian. On March 18, St. Joseph's Eve, the club hosted a ball at Odd Fellows' Hall attended by more than two hundred members. The next day started with a mass followed by members parading in the streets with a brass band, stopping at homes along the route. The day ended with a dinner at the nearby Younger's (or Young's) Hall.[25] The next year, the Società expanded its celebration and was recognized as a "well-known and influential society composed of prominent Italians." It not only raised funds for its tomb in St. Louis Cemetery #1 but also paraded through the Fourth and Sixth Districts, followed by a banquet and ball at the Majestic Hall on Magazine and Sixth Streets: "Guests were present from the Italian colony, and also from the American friends of the society."[26] The community embraced St. Joseph's Eve as a uniquely Creole New Orleans-style mid-Lent celebration, blending it with their traditional religious observance of St. Joseph.

In 1912, the Sicilian altars of New Orleans first appeared in the local press alongside listings for other celebrations: "Every (Sicilian) home, humble and pretentious, erected an altar in honor of the earthly father of Jesus, and on it was a vast assortment of wine, cakes, candies and dozens of other delicacies." The worship service "was crowded with hundreds of Italian working men and women." An altar in the corner of the church was specially decorated with candles.[27]

The altars that Sicilians created for St. Joseph's Day stand out as one of the city's most enduring tributes to its culture. These enormous altars are laden with food, flowers, photos honoring the deceased, and symbols commemorating the immigrants' lives in New Orleans and their past in the old country. Their placement and structure embody the number three, reflecting the Holy Trinity. Ethelyn Orso identified three types of altars: altars built in private homes, those found in commercial spaces such as sweet shops or restaurants, and large altars funded and maintained by churches, institutions, or organizations. Although these altars differ in appearance, they are usually constructed with three tiers, often with a statue of Saint Joseph at the top; the altars are usually surrounded by blessed palm leaves, flowers, or greenery. Many feature the colors of the Italian flag—green, white, and red—and others display the primary colors of the Sicilian flag, red and yellow. Labors of love, these altars exhibit vibrant textiles and artistically arranged displays of food, offered to visitors both as sustenance for the body and as symbols to nourish the soul.

Altars are typically constructed for three reasons. Many serve to express a petition, for example, a cure for a sick individual. They are also built in gratitude for a blessing received through the intercession of St. Joseph or to honor the recently deceased.[28] For example, Nicolas Rouse expressed his gratitude to St. Joseph in a *New Orleans Item* personal ad labeled "Faith." He believed the saint's intervention had saved his leg after an accident in 1893, and he continued to erect an altar in his home for the next twenty-four years in thanksgiving.[29]

Decorating an altar is a deeply personal act. A statue of St. Joseph is often placed in a prominent position at its top, front, or center; it is accompanied by candles, flags, greenery, and flowers, particularly lilies that bloom around his feast day. Statues of doves, other saints, and Sicilian folk art are

A St. Joseph's altar in New Orleans, 1930. Residence of Mrs. Frank Gennaro on Gov. Nicholls Street. WPA Papers, State Library of Louisiana, Wp001566.

interspersed with photographs of those who have passed and are being remembered. Tables are filled with plates of food—except for meat, because it is Lent—baked sweets, and raw produce. In baskets scattered about are breads baked in fantastical shapes with Christian symbolism, such as fish, ladders, crosses, and hearts. Cooked fish, fennel, artichokes both raw and stuffed, almonds, cakes, and cookies in all shapes and colors, especially *cuccidati,* complete the spread. *Cuccidati* are the famous fig cookies that are found in the "goody bags" given to those who visit the altar. Along with the cookies, visitors receive a St. Joseph prayer card, a blessed fava bean, and a piece of bread. The blessed piece of bread is believed to calm a storm when thrown into it, and many trust that if they carry the fava bean in their wallet or purse, they will never want for anything.

Many Sicilian Catholics who later moved from Louisiana continue the spiritual tradition of building altars on St. Joseph's Day. There is ample evidence that as people migrated elsewhere they established a "trail of the St. Joseph altar," spreading the tradition across the nation and promoting the public display of the holiday by Sicilians and other ethnic groups.

The most widely accepted origin story for the altars holds that they were first erected after a famine in Sicily. After the famine ended, the people wanted to express their gratitude for the saint's intervention, which ended their suffering, and also to show their appreciation for the humble fava bean, which nourished the starving people. These themes of petition and gratitude continue in the altars today.[30] According to an alternative legend, "in the Middle Ages, a group of Sicilians were exiled from their country and set adrift on the sea in a small boat. In despair, they prayed to St. Joseph for guidance and protection, promising to honor him each year if their lives were spared. Cast upon the shore of an uninhabited island, they immediately erected an altar of branches and palmetto leaves and decorated it with wisteria, wild red lilies, and other flowers."[31]

Begging for money and for items to place on the altar is another tradition that many follow; it reflects the Holy Family's poverty at the time of Jesus's birth. For many, begging is the foundation of their altar, and giving to those in need is the outcome. When the altar is "broken" or taken down, the food is given to the less fortunate. Donations and gifts from neighborhood residents create a "feast table that was a communal affair."[32]

Paul Coniglio recalled that he and his wife Catarina created their first altar in 1906 after Catarina had taken ill. She had taken medicines that the doctor prescribed, but they believed that "it only St. Joseph that mak'a Catarina cure!" So, she promised to make an altar to St. Joseph on his feast day by begging for contributions and asking for assistance because St. Joseph appeared to her in a dream and told her, "You musta beg fo' the altar mon' an' aska at least three people." She did receive some help but ultimately decided to pay for everything and build the altar herself. Her husband explained that some people made a spectacle of begging and were given a lot of money, which they kept for themselves. He said, "My family no lika that," and in 1940, at the time of the interview, they had been building their altar for thirty-four years.[33] During the Depression, one woman proclaimed that she never begged but that people nevertheless donated flour, sugar, or money.[34]

Most of the Sicilians who came to New Orleans after escaping famine and oppression were peasants who had cultivated the land. This experience of famine led to their intense "preoccupations with food," which they used to symbolize their ethnicity and express gratitude.[35] Food represented earthly bounty, known as *abbondanza* in Italian, as well as the feast that awaits Catholics in the afterlife. Altars reflected the bountiful life they found in their new home. Their hunger for food was fulfilled by the rich, fertile soil of the Mississippi Delta, in which they grew vegetables. More importantly, they became grocers and manufacturers of specialty items, such as pasta—all the products that still adorn the altars today.

Altars also became symbols of their culture and allowed them to invite their new neighbors into their homes to celebrate life's great pleasures, such as eating and sharing food together. They were originally "closed," signifying the "identity containment and exclusion of outside groups that characterized the behavior in the enclaves of various immigrant ethnic groups"; the earliest altars were likely private. But by the 1910s, they were "open" to friends or those who understood the entrance sign, which was a palm frond over the door.[36]

A St. Joseph's altar in New Orleans, March 19, 1942. Residence of Mrs. Foto on St. Philip Street. WPA Papers, State Library of Louisiana, Wp001574.

On March 20, 1917, just a few weeks before the United States joined the Allied forces to fight against the Central powers, the *Times-Picayune* published a detailed account of an altar adorned with decorative loaves of bread, flowers, candles, and palms; the excellent menu included "macaroni and parched bread, spaghetti, rice fritters, the especial fast-day food of St. Joseph, even in North Italy, dried chestnuts, called castagne; cauliflower omelet, stuffed artichoke stems, anchovies, finecchio, or anise omelet, stuffed olives and black olives, green horse beans, dried figs and clusters of dough-almonds which had been fried and rolled in honey and which tasted like Italian skies, the Blue Grotto, and almonds."[37] Many boys and men from the New Orleans area enlisted in World War I, a number comparable to those in other communities nationwide. Those who stayed behind ensured that dedications on the altars during the war years included soldiers, increasing local interest in the altars. Many families understandably prayed to St. Joseph for the safe return of their sons and husbands. The altars not only promoted solidarity within the Sicilian community but also strengthened ties to many non-Sicilian residents who attended, praying for the safety of their own family members.

As men returned to their families in New Orleans after the war, the Sicilians knew precisely how to show their gratitude for the mercy they had received: they continued to build altars in St. Joseph's honor. These altars and the day's celebration became a widely accepted tradition, blending into the city's existing St. Joseph's Day festivities. In 1919, the *Times-Picayune* published an article listing altars in the surrounding area, revealing an "unprecedented number of altars" honoring St. Joseph due to the "victorious ending to the war." The article mentioned that hundreds of altars were erected throughout the city on this day and that thousands of people had visited a single family's altar, shifting the focus of St. Joseph's Day's from festivities to more religious, Sicilian-style observances. However, celebrations on St. Joseph's Day are "not restricted to this nationality" but include "entertainments of various kinds."[38]

During this transitional period, some New Orleanians connected the two observances through music. Johnny Provenzano, a musician, recounted that from 1907 until he left New Orleans to serve in World War I, he played at the dedication of twelve St. Joseph's Eve altars, and on St. Joseph's Eve, he performed church music, highlighting how Sicilian Americans contributed to the Creole tradition of St. Joseph's Day as mid-Lent.[39] However, the next night, "there was usually a St. Joseph's ball or dance somewhere, and we would play jazz all evening."

Around this time, jazz would have another, more gruesome connection to St. Joseph's Day. In 1919, a serial killer had murdered several Sicilians, and St. Joseph's Day marked a grim turning point in his terrorizing the city's residents. The "Axman of New Orleans," notorious for using an ax in his murders, allegedly sent a bizarre letter to a local newspaper stating that at 12:15 a.m. on Tuesday, March 19, he would "pass over New Orleans," asserting that "every person shall be spared in whose house a jazz band is in full swing." Many residents "found in it inspiration for house parties with jazz music having a prominent place on the program," or perhaps they were merely celebrating St. Joseph's Day as they had for years.[40] A masquerade ball for St. Joseph's Day took place on the upper floor of the French Union Hall; however, none of these St. Joseph's dances mentioned the "Axman." The "Axman" was never caught, and the murders remain unsolved to this day.

Although the Sicilian community continued to celebrate their ethnicity and the blessings from St. Joseph as proud New Orleanians with their altars, prejudice persisted until the early 1920s. They were blamed for being "tenants in poor circumstances," and in the French Market, they were viewed as "hucksters" who brought about "a regrettable but significant change."[41] The personal advertisements in the back of the newspaper became the place to find listings for the altars. Nestled between the notices about lost dogs and ads for palm readers, information about their locations could be found.[42] And by 1928, it was noted that "visiting altars on St. Joseph's Eve is an established custom here" as "symbolical of adoration, laden with good things to eat and drink." Many even believed that those who visited nine altars in one night had their wishes come true.[43]

St. Joseph's Day altars highlighted the community's strength and solidarity and was a way to connect to their Black neighbors. Additionally, Black Spiritual churches embraced the holiday and its altar tradition.

Black Spiritual churches came to New Orleans in 1918 when a strong and charismatic woman named Leafy Anderson moved there to establish the first of its kind. Soon after, St. Joseph's Day became one of the most significant feast days on its calendar of events.[44] According to Anderson, Rev. Maude Shannon was the first Black person to organize a St. Joseph altar: "We has our altar on St. Joseph's Night just like the 'talian people, and we gives away all our food to everybody what comes." The altar, built by her congregation, included "all the Italian foods along with stuffed eggs and potato salad." In 1938, she celebrated St. Joseph's Day with a feast at the Daniel Helping Hand Divine Spiritual Church, where she was pastor.[45] In an interview, she revealed that she met St. Joseph, and he told her to use her rent money to build an altar. She continued, "I was scared I never

A St. Joseph's altar in New Orleans, 1930s. Residence of B. B. Montalbano on St. Philip Street. Photo by Erol Barkemeyer. WPA Papers, State Library of Louisiana, Wp001568.

would get my rent together again," but she had faith, and her first altar was created.

However, the first St. Joseph's Day altar at a Spiritual church was reported to be in 1928 at Lena Scovotto's Sacred Heart Spiritual Church. The church created "one of the largest altars in the city" and, before the distribution of food, held a "procession of saints" consisting of local children dressed as saints and angels.[46] Scovotto was one of Leafy Anderson's closest friends. Her 1928 voter registration confirmed that she was not Black but Sicilian. She listed her birth parish as Palermo and boldly changed her occupation from housewife to "Reverend," crossing out the traditional prefixes to add her own.[47] Following her friend's lead, she founded a Spiritual church, and by 1941, she designated Sacred Heart Spiritual Church as her place of employment.[48]

Mother Catherine Seals, another protégée of Mother Leafy, managed the Temple of the Innocent Blood on Charbonnet Street in the Lower Ninth Ward. She preached in her integrated church to both Black and white residents, particularly Sicilian immigrants, until she passed away in the 1930s.[49] Sicilians were notoriously suspicious of the Catholic Church, given centuries of mistreatment in their homeland. At the same time, Black New Orleanians often adapted Catholicism to fulfill needs overlooked by white religious officials. Both groups were wary of going to orthodox clergy for spiritual guidance because of their established societal roles and turned instead to spiritual churches for support.

Many Spiritual churches continued to honor the tradition of altars on St. Joseph's Day throughout the 1940s and likely beyond. In 1994, a reporter visited a St. Joseph's Day altar at a Black Spiritual church, where he found a loaf of still-wrapped Wonder Bread in place of the traditional Italian breads, alongside sacks of beans and rice. These foods were gathered from various stores, maintaining the Sicilian tradition but without the fava beans, thereby demonstrating a fusion of cultures with necessary adaptations.[50] St. Joseph's Day became a point of connection and interchange that Sicilian and Black city residents explored together.

In 1940, St. Joseph's Day fell during Holy Week, prompting Archbishop Rummel to instruct the city to celebrate it on April 2. The responses of Sicilians who took part in the St. Joseph's Day celebrations mirrored those of their Black neighbors. Some accepted the new date, whereas others were outraged. The altars should have been allowed during Holy Week because the Sicilians were celebrating a saint's feast day rather than mid-Lent; however, by the 1940s, the history of the celebrations had become muddled. On the street next to the racetrack, a bar owner discovered that its altar had been denied a proper blessing over the years because it was located in a drinking establishment. The priest who refused the request that year, Monsignor Racine, later pointed out that perhaps it was not so much the altars but that on St. Joseph's Day, "some people dance, some marry on St. Joseph's Day. The Church sometimes has a celebration. We cannot have that through Holy Week, so we will follow the Bishop's rule." The proprietor quickly responded, "We don't dance," reiterating that the bar's St. Joseph's Day was on the saint's feast day—a holy day. However, a Filipina resident near Bayou St. John recalled that a church usually held dances on St. Joseph's Night, which ended at midnight. Those dances seem more like mid-Lent festivities than the Sicilian-inspired altars, but it is unclear which church she referred to.

Many questioned the calendar change because the pope had not made this decision; instead, it came from local authorities. Some outright ignored it, revealing long-standing rifts between the Sicilians and the Catholic Church. Although Sicilians were Catholic, they often infused their practices with interpretations and elements that many considered superstitions, such as carrying a fava bean blessed at a St. Joseph's Day altar, known as a lucky bean, and wearing the *cornetto,* or Italian horn, for protection and good luck. They felt a strong obligation to honor the saint with whom they had a personal connection and did not hesitate to ignore the archbishop's order.

Specifically, Mrs. Christina announced that she would get her altar blessed if she had to "drag the priest out by-a the neck." If he refused, she would "get some Holy Water and get-a one of those real old-a Italians that know the old prayer and blessa her altar, not on April 2, it willa be March 19,

A St. Joseph's altar in New Orleans, April 2, 1940. Residence of Mrs. R. Caparo on Magazine Street. WPA Papers, State Library of Louisiana, Wp001586.

St. Joseph's Day."[51] Jokingly, many called that second feast "the archbishop's St. Joseph's Day."[52] Another Sicilian woman proclaimed that if the priest would not bless her altar, she would "take a the bottle to the Church, get some Holy Water, stand-a back here like this, sprinkle-a the water, say a prayer to St. Joseph, myself and save-a the dollar."[53]

Others supported the archbishop's decision. Mrs. P. Messina from 3326 St. Claude Avenue, said, "I think it was wrong for some-a the peoples who have Altars on the nineteenth this year; it only happens every fifty years St. Joseph day come in Holy week and like the priest, explain to me, if you-a gonna have a wedding and some one-a die in the house you postpone, well the church was in mourning, draped in purple, how could they have Altars."[54] By 1952, altars had become so common that a brief description in the *New Orleans Item* was accompanied by a reminder that "interested persons may find locations of St. Joseph's altars through the *Item* want ad columns."[55]

A St. Joseph's altar in New Orleans, 1930s. Residence of Mrs. J. Quagliano on Gov. Nicholls Street. WPA Papers, State Library of Louisiana, Wp001567.

In 1967, New Orleanians commemorated St. Joseph's Day on March 18 because Palm Sunday occurred that year on March 19. Mayor Victor Schiro, of Sicilian heritage, formally acknowledged the occasion with a morning mass at St. Joseph's Church and organized an afternoon parade from City Hall to the church, where an outdoor altar was duly established. Later that evening, the Greater New Orleans Italian Cultural Society held a banquet at the Jung Hotel.[56] Attention in the local newspapers and the participation of city officials sharply contrasted with the minimal coverage of the 1940 date change, indicating a shift in the standing of the Sicilian community.

By the 1960s, the Sicilian American residents feared that their traditions were being lost. The blame was placed squarely on "intermarriage and a failure on the part of the older Italians to pass down traditions have caused a local falling away from St. Joseph."[57] In 1968, the *Times-Picayune*'s pullout section, *Dixie Magazine,* ran a full spread on the local tradition of St. Joseph's Day, explaining that "local touches make its New Orleans celebration different from similar events across the country and in Europe where heavy ceramic statues of the saints are borne on the shoulders of young men. In New Orleans, the statue is made of papier mâché and mounted on a float, Mardi Gras style, for better viewing by the public." By then Sicilians had been accepted into much of white society, with one blatant exception: Carnival krewes. For the most part, they were not invited to participate in Carnival balls until the latter part of the twentieth century, so these parades became an essential part of Sicilian St. Joseph's Day celebrations in New Orleans to fill that gap.

In 1969, Sicilians, now mostly called Italians, celebrated their third annual St. Joseph's Day parade, "Irish Channel Style," through the uptown neighborhood named for those from the Emerald Isle who had settled there. By then the parade had evolved to include floats, marching clubs, jazz bands, and doubloons that were thrown, much like those during Carnival parades; one float featured an illuminated statue of St. Joseph. An individual named Messina marched with a "large stick of ripe bananas as a *shillelagh*—Italian style."[58] These festivities resembled the earlier public parades that had faded after the Hennessy incident. Thus, St. Joseph's Day came to combine sacred Sicilian ideals with secular, carnival-like mid-Lent celebrations.[59]

These parades soon evolved into a festive masculine alternative to the women-decorated altars. They also highlighted Italian ethnicity, boldly marching through public spaces, no longer confined to homes and semi-public places like restaurants and grocery stores. These parades symbolize the evolution of Sicilian St. Joseph's Day celebrations in New Orleans and reflect the idea that "non-religious ethnic festivals are the primary source for celebrating heritage in the United States. The religious ethnic festivals that have lasted for centuries continue to thrive, but with added emphasis on the ethnic aspect."[60] Many people still visit altars, but parades now attract both locals and tourists alike.

In 1972, the "old French Quarter took on a definite Italian flavor Saturday night" thanks to the second annual Italian American Marching Club parade. This Carnival-style parade featured "five marching bands, decorated carriages and pony carts, a St. Joseph Altar float and two floats depicting Italian gondolas carrying maids of the organization dressed in imported Italian costumes." The evening concluded with a spaghetti and meatball dinner at St. Mary's gym.[61] Serving meat was an addition to the holiday that was only mentioned in this one account and indicates that this event blurred the line between the two celebrations of mid-Lent and the feast day of the saint.

Today, the Italian American Parade is the only night parade featuring full-sized floats that continues to traverse the French Quarter.[62] It attracts Italian Americans from the entertainment industry beyond New Orleans, including past grand marshals like Tony Bennett and James Gandolfini. In 1977, the parade started and ended at the Municipal Auditorium and was dubbed "probably the most striking Old-World parade" as it wound through the French Quarter. In 1979, grand marshal Robert Goulet joined the Irish to toast with green beer and Chianti on Esplanade Avenue, marking the first and possibly last such encounter on Royal and Esplanade Streets and showcasing floats representing the Italian provinces (note: not Sicilian).[63]

This parade led to others in the city's suburbs celebrating the Italian heritage and sometimes teaming up with the Irish, likely because St. Patrick's Day falls only two days before St. Joseph's Day. Other new traditions emerged, such as stealing a lemon from an altar without getting caught. St. Francis Xavier Church in Metairie addressed the lemon controversy: "Stealing a lemon has several interpretations. Stealing a lemon from an altar and leaving money for the poor is said to be good luck. Others say a blessed lemon stolen from the altar will not turn black. The most popular interpretation is that stealing a lemon and not getting caught will ensure you will be married."[64] This tradition is troublesome to many who worry that it reinforces the stereotype of Sicilians as dishonest and thieves.

Not only is St. Joseph honored with an abundance of fruits and vegetables on his altars but the day has also become a reliable time to start planting crops outdoors. Many Sicilian Americans recognize this day as the right time to plant in the ground, because the risk of a freeze has passed. The saint is regarded as "a kind of protector for one's crops, a sort of frost-proofer," particularly for the lucky fava bean.[65]

In the years following Hurricane Katrina, concerns emerged about the persistence of the city's many traditions, particularly the St. Joseph's Day altars. Nevertheless, celebrations for St. Joseph's Day flourished. Parades continued, and the number of altars appearing throughout the city and its suburbs increased. Although some homes display altars, others are now showcased by restaurants, bars, bakeries, grocery stores, schools, churches, and even cemeteries, many of which lack Sicilian roots. Today, many New Orleanians from various backgrounds participate in St. Joseph's Day festivities by visiting altars and engaging with the local community. This growing acceptance of St. Joseph's Day celebrations, an unquenchable desire for local festivals, and the next generation of Sicilian New Orleanians' passion for traditional customs have revitalized the St. Joseph's Day altars. By sharing their food and culture, these immigrants left their mark on the city that became one of the world's culinary capitals.

Enrique Alférez lithograph for March in a calendar series. Enrique Alférez, *Twelve Months of New Orleans—March 1940,* color lithograph. Ogden Museum of Southern Art, Gift of the Roger H. Ogden Collection. 2003.1.12 @TlalocAlférez.

CONCLUSION

Without the history and the neighborhoods,
the culture has no content. Without the culture,
the neighborhoods have no spirit.
—KEITH WELDON MEDLEY, *Black Life in Old New Orleans*

New Orleans Black Creole poet Sybil Kein paints a picture of "children in their white dresses and suits" visiting their Sicilian neighbors and enjoying the food from their bountiful altars: "little sandwiches, stuffed eggs, breads, black olives, honey candies, and big lucky beans."[1] She explicitly references Black Creole children, emphasizing that by the 1980s, visiting St. Joseph's Day altars had become an integral part of Black Creole culture in New Orleans. Four of her *Nine Rites of the Creole* are sacraments of the Catholic Church: Baptism, First Communion, marriage, and burial. The others are "so common to South Louisiana" that they "have a sacramental force sanctioned by communities: St. Joseph's Day, All Saints, when graves are cleaned and decorated; Christmas and New Year's, and of course; finally, a wake, which is a subdued reunion of family and friends."[2]

According to Kein, Mardi Gras is a tradition, whereas St. Joseph's Day is a rite. However, in its original form as mid-Lent, St. Joseph's Day might have been viewed as a tradition. Over time, it gained significance in the Creole community as a Catholic rite, primarily because of its adoption by Sicilians as the feast of St. Joseph. As a result, St. Joseph's Day has become a key part of the city's culture and one of the few remaining symbols of Sicilian heritage in a predominantly Creole environment. Both interpretations of the day are essential for understanding the city's history and highlight the once strong connection between these two groups, which were both previously marginalized.

Along with Mardi Gras, St. Joseph's Day as mid-Lent served as an important reminder for early settlers of their Catholic Frenchness in the uncharted territories of colonial Louisiana during both French and later Spanish rule. Both holidays acted as unifying symbols for everyone, regardless of race. After the Louisiana Purchase and during the early years of statehood, Mardi Gras emerged as the primary celebration for wealthy white Anglo-Americans, relegating St. Joseph's Day to a lesser status: it was then mainly recognized by a few specific groups, rather than the broader community. Amid rising racial tensions, the Anglo participants used Mardi Gras traditions to assert a clearer racial identity, leaving St. Joseph's Day to become a celebration specifically for Black New Orleanians as mid-Lent.

Holidays, of course, are occasions for enjoyment and celebration. However, a deeper examination reveals that they often serve as reflections of their historical and cultural contexts. The history of St. Joseph's Day in New Orleans highlights the profound impact of race in shaping the city's social structure and its societal implications. It provides a valuable perspective for exploring complex concepts of race, its impact, and its enduring legacy. St. Joseph's Day continued relevance is underpinned by a strong dedication to safeguarding vital cultural traditions.

Over time, St. Joseph's Day and the Black Masking Indians became powerful symbols of cultural pride, vividly showcased in their appearances throughout the neighborhoods. Surprisingly, Sicilian immigrants and their descendants emerged as unexpected allies, feeding the Black Masking Indians both literally and figuratively. Other Sicilian celebrations disappeared, but the altars remain a direct representation of Sicilians in New Orleans. Many Sicilians who embraced this holiday used it to gain recognition and acceptance, inviting their neighbors to share in the fruits of their labor and joy.

Many members of the Black and Sicilian communities of New Orleans created and upheld the rituals associated with St. Joseph's Day. The resources available to them and the strong sense of community it provided allowed these traditions to endure and thrive as they do today. Both Sicilians and Black residents found common ground in the neighborhoods where they settled, as well as in their shared low social status. By fostering a shared culture of celebrations on St. Joseph's Day, Black New Orleanians transformed into Indians, while the newer immigrants, acting as guardians of their roots, shared their preserved culture. The rituals of these two marginalized groups, the Black New Orleanians and those of Sicilian descent, ensured that St. Joseph's Day in New Orleans persisted in both forms.

The evolution of St. Joseph's Day in New Orleans reflects a city struggling with racial tensions yet managing to address them in surprising ways. Segregation was enforced by finding social outlets to calm the population. Race greatly influenced life in New Orleans, a city that often presented itself as carefree and tolerant but was often cruel and prejudiced. The joy that emerged from marginalized groups' oppression was transformed into the glory of the Black Masking Indians and the joyous altars of Sicilian Americans. Neither group let their standing in life nor lack of wealth stop them from expressing themselves.

In sharing traditions, barriers were broken, and both communities overcame the dangers of poverty and oppression, even if only for one day. These parallel rituals helped build a community rooted in available resources—food for the Sicilians and beautifully designed Indian suits for their neighbors. A forgotten holiday continued and was transformed into a vibrant celebration of gratitude. For traditions to last, there must be respect and connections. Long ago, these two groups found this in their neighbors.

Notes

1. CREATING A CREOLE HOLIDAY

1. Gray, "Rediscovering the 'Antiguo Cementerio,'" 228.
2. O'Gorman, "Canada's Patron Saint," 5.
3. Le Clercq, *First Establishment of the Faith in New France,* 223.
4. O'Gorman, "Canada's Patron Saint," 648–49.
5. Greer, *The Jesuit Relations,* 117.
6. Falconer, *On the Discovery of the Mississippi,* 5.
7. Le Clercq, *First Establishment,* 20.
8. Iberville, *Iberville's Gulf Journals,* 74.
9. Jones, *The Shattered Cross,* 41–42.
10. Johnson, "Colonial New Orleans," 30.
11. Hall, *Africans in Colonial Louisiana,* 14
12. DeJean, *Mutinous Women,* 162, 166.
13. Johnson, "Colonial New Orleans," 19.
14. Powell, *The Accidental City,* 97.
15. Barthé, *Becoming American in Creole New Orleans,* 12.
16. Reed, "The Myth of Authenticity and Its Impact on Politics," 310–12.
17. Johnson, "Vodou Purchase," 151.
18. Guenin-Lelle, *Story of French New Orleans,* 100.
19. Long, "New Orleans as an American City," 203–22.
20. Spear, *Race, Sex, and Social Order in Early New Orleans,* 216.
21. Hall, *Africans in Colonial Louisiana,* 5.
22. DeJean, *Mutinous Women,* 1–2.
23. Eccles, *France in America,* 170.
24. Bell, "French Religious Culture in Afro-Creole New Orleans," 9.
25. Twitty, *The Cooking Gene,* 192.
26. Guenin-Lelle, *Story of French New Orleans,* 47.

27. Hall, *Africans in Colonial Louisiana,* 238.

28. DeJean, *Mutinous Women,* 351.

29. Hall, *Africans in Colonial Louisiana,* 336.

30. Dudley, *Building Antebellum New Orleans,* 156.

31. New Orleans Archdiocese correspondence, September 1799, University of Notre Dame Archives.

32. New Orleans Archdiocese correspondence, April 20, 26, 1786, University of Notre Dame Archives.

33. New Orleans Archdiocese correspondence, October 20, 1792, University of Notre Dame Archives.

34. Pastor, "Black Catholicism," 18, 2.

35. Hall, *Africans in Colonial Louisiana,* 157–58.

36. Parham, *American Routes,* 78.

37. Long, "New Orleans," 218–21.

38. Stewart, "Spirituality and Resistance Among African Creoles," 185.

39. Dudley, *Building Antebellum New Orleans,* 25.

40. Faber, *Building the Land of Dreams,* 122.

41. Homans, *Apollo's Angels,* 32.

42. Greer, *The Jesuit Relations,* 61.

43. New Orleans Archdiocese correspondence, 1790s, University of Notre Dame Archives.

44. Posey, Federal Writers' Project Papers, folder 44, Cammie G. Henry Research Center, Northwestern State University of Louisiana.

45. New Orleans Archdiocese correspondence, January 9, 1801, University of Notre Dame Archives.

46. DeJean, *Mutinous Women,* 332.

47. WPA Papers, State Library of Louisiana, March 20, 1907, wp005476.

48. *Daily City Item,* February 9, 1891.

49. Young, *The Mistick Krewe,* 3–5.

50. Tallant, *The Romantic New Orleanians,* 123.

51. Kmen, *Music in New Orleans,* 8.

52. Busi, "Flaubert's Use of Saints' Names in Madame Bovary," 99–100.

53. Sante, *The Other Paris,* 132–3.

54. Flint, *Recollections of the Last Ten Years,* 309.

55. Parham, *American Routes,* 69.

56. Blassingame, *Black New Orleans, 1860–1880,* xvi.

57. Parham, *American Routes,* 92.

58. Taylor, *Louisiana Reconstructed, 1863–1877,* 5–6.

59. Taylor, *Louisiana Reconstructed,* 446–51.

60. Saxon, *Gumbo Ya-Ya,* 99.

2. COLONIAL CELEBRATIONS

1. Kmen, *Music in New Orleans,* 3, 10–11.

2. Hanger, *Bounded Lives, Bounded Places,* 9.

3. DeJean, *Mutinous Women,* 14.

4. Johnson, "Colonial New Orleans," 45.

5. LaCour, *New Orleans Masquerade,* 8.

6. Caillot, *A Company Man,* 134–36.

7. Latrobe, *Southern Travels,* 78.

8. DeJean, *Mutinous Women,* 250.

9. Hachard, *The Letters of Marie Madeleine Hachard,* 17, 55.

10. Osborne, *Mardi Gras!,* 42.

11. Ebeyer, *Paramours of the Creoles,* 152–53.

12. Hachard, *Letters of Marie Madeleine Hachard,* 58.

13. Kinser, *Carnival, American Style,* 17.

14. Johnson, "Versailles, Meet Les Halles," 89.

15. Atkins, *New Orleans Carnival Balls,* 12.

16. Blassingame, *Black New Orleans,* 3.

17. Hall, *Africans in Colonial Louisiana,* 241.

18. Hall, *Africans in Colonial Louisiana,* xiv–xv.

19. Wegmann, "The Vitriolic Blood of a Negro," 210.

20. Vidal, *Caribbean New Orleans,* 201.

21. Harvey, *Christianity and Race in the American South,* 41.

22. Powell, *The Accidental City,* 141.

23. Biagetti, "Enlightenment and Revolution," 69–84.

24. Gotham, *Authentic New Orleans,* 24.

25. WPA Papers, State Library of Louisiana; Cabildo Book #2, New Orleans City Hall Archives, September 8, 1669–June 25, 1784.

26. Couch, "Public Masked Balls of Antebellum New Orleans," 406.

27. Powell, *The Accidental City,* 220.

28. Kmen, *Music in New Orleans,* 16–17.

29. Hanger, *Bounded Lives, Bounded Places,* 143.

30. Johnson, "Urban Development and the Culture of Masked Balls," 648.

31. Johnson, "Versailles, Meet Les Halles," 96–99, 112.

32. Parham, *American Routes,* 138–39.

33. Schindler, *Mardi Gras,* 17.

34. Powell, *The Accidental City,* 220.

35. Faber, *Building the Land of Dreams,* 57.

36. Kinser, *Carnival, American Style,* 24–25.

37. An interesting side note: in 1795 Filiberto Farge requested a land grant for two of the

lots of the St. Peter Street Cemetery. He was denied, but perhaps his intention was to build a ballroom on top of the old cemetery. Gray, "Rediscovering the 'Antiguo Cementerio,'" 24.

38. Le Gardeur, *The First New Orleans Theatre,* 2, 4, 13, 6.

39. Holmes, *A Guide to Spanish Louisiana,* 21.

40. Guenin-Lelle, *Story of French New Orleans,* 113.

41. Vidal, *Caribbean New Orleans,* 169–70.

42. Letter from Almonaster Estrada, New Orleans Archdiocese correspondence, February 5, 1795, University of Notre Dame Archives.

43. Teja, "St. James at the Fair," 395–416.

44. Hanger, *Bounded Lives, Bounded Places,* 142.

45. Cuming, *Sketches of a Tour to the Western Country,* 336.

46. Kinser, *Carnival, American Style,* 70–71.

47. Hanger, *Bounded Lives, Bounded Places,* 142, 145.

48. Aslakson, *Making Race in the Courtroom,* 122.

49. Kinser, *Carnival, American Style,* 25–26.

50. Kmen, *Music in New Orleans,* 43–46.

51. Morazan, "'Quadroon' Balls in the Spanish Period," 311–15.

52. Kinser, *Carnival, American Style,* 25–26.

53. Hanger, *Bounded Lives, Bounded Places,* 136–38, 147.

54. Powell, *The Accidental City,* 312.

55. Aslakson, *Making Race in the Courtroom,* 78, 83.

56. Laussat, *Memoirs of My Life,* 55, 119.

57. Carpentier, *Kingdom of This World,* 56.

58. Berquin-Duvallon, *Travels in Louisiana and the Floridas,* 47, 48.

59. Castellanos, *New Orleans as It Was,* 160.

60. Atkins, *New Orleans Carnival Balls,* 16.

61. Johnson, "Colonial New Orleans," 45.

62. Laussat, *Memoirs of My Life,* 18.

63. Robertson, *Louisiana Under the Rule of Spain, France, and the United States,* 33.

64. Pitot, *Observations on the Colony of Louisiana,* 29, 36.

65. Robin, *Voyage to Louisiana,* 56–57.

3. ANTEBELLUM ST. JOSEPH'S DAY

1. Faber, *Building the Land of Dreams,* 145.

2. Claiborne, *Official Letter Books,* 322, 327.

3. Laussat, *Memoirs of My Life,* 92–93.

4. Claiborne, *Official Letter Books,* 329.

5. Parham, *American Routes,* 74.

6. Faber, *Building the Land of Dreams,* 158.

7. Laussat, *Memoirs of My Life,* 94–96.

8. Claiborne, *Official Letter Books,* 352–55.

9. Faber, *Building the Land of Dreams,* 161.

10. Wall and Rodrigue, *Louisiana: A History,* 123–24.

11. Castellanos, *New Orleans as It Was,* 161.

12. Letter from Jean Etienne de Boré to Thomas Jefferson, February 10, 1804, National Archives—Founders Online, https://founders.archives.gov/documents/Jefferson/01-42-02-0378.

13. Couch, "Public Masked Balls," 408.

14. Kmen, *Music in New Orleans,* 3.

15. Robin, *Voyage to Louisiana,* 64.

16. Claiborne, *Official Letter Books,* 388.

17. Rien, "Charles Gayarré and the Imagining of an Exceptional City," 61.

18. Olmsted, *A Journey in the Seaboard Slave States,* 580.

19. Parham, *American Routes,* 95.

20. Brook, *The Accident of Color,* 8.

21. Crutcher, *Tremé,* 25.

22. Faber, *Building the Land of Dreams,* 235–42.

23. Hall, *Africans in Colonial Louisiana,* 241. Although there was a class of free people of color in Saint-Domingue, their racial social structure was rigid, unlike in New Orleans.

24. Brook, *The Accident of Color,* 21–23.

25. Gotham, *Authentic New Orleans,* 24.

26. Kmen, *Music in New Orleans,* 34–6.

27. Couch, "Public Masked Balls," 408–11.

28. Dessens, *From Saint-Domingue to New Orleans,* 27.

29. Hall, *Social Control in Slave Plantation Societies,* 126.

30. Stewart, "Spirituality and Resistance," 185.

31. Vidal, *Caribbean New Orleans,* 511.

32. Ferrer, *Freedom's Mirror,* 1, 17.

33. DeJean, *Mutinous Women,* 170.

34. Dessens, *From Saint-Domingue to New Orleans,* 70.

35. Dessens, *From Saint-Domingue to New Orleans,* 1, 40.

36. Dessens, *From Saint-Domingue to New Orleans,* 1, 40, 158.

37. *Le Moniteur,* March 18, 1807; *Le Moniteur,* March 16, 1808.

38. Gotham, *Authentic New Orleans,* 24.

39. Couch, "Public Masked Balls," 415.

40. Couch, Public Masked Balls," 410–16.

41. *Le Courier,* March 5, 1824.

42. *Louisiana State Gazette,* March 20, 1824.
43. *Louisiana State Gazette,* March 8, 1824.
44. Couch, "Public Masked Balls," 413.
45. Flint, *Recollections of the Last Ten Years,* 274, 307, 310.
46. Dessens, *Creole City,* 28.
47. Gotham, *Authentic New Orleans,* 17, 24.
48. Hirsch and Logsdon, *Creole New Orleans,* 91.
49. Cowan and McGuire, *Louisiana Governors,* 61.
50. Johnson, "Colonial New Orleans," 46.
51. Crété, *Daily Life in Louisiana,* 204–6.
52. LaCour, *New Orleans Masquerade,* 10.
53. Dunn, "Mardi Gras in New Orleans."
54. Fischer, *The Segregation Struggle in Louisiana,* 17–18.
55. *New Orleans Bee,* March 19, 1828.
56. Radestock, *Royal Ball-Room Guide,* 37.
57. Dessens, *Creole City,* 94.
58. Dudley, *Building Antebellum New Orleans,* 11.
59. *L'Abeille,* March 19, 1829.
60. *L'Abeille,* March 17, 1830.
61. Kmen, *Music in New Orleans,* 15.
62. *L'Abeille,* March 19, 1833.
63. Dessens, *Creole City,* 44.
64. Flint, *Recollections of the Last Ten Years,* 336.
65. Hurston, *Mules and Men,* 192.
66. Latrobe, *Southern Travels,* 56.
67. Latrobe, *Southern Travels,* 76–80.
68. Aslakson, *Making Race in the Courtroom,* 125.
69. Guenin-Lelle, *Story of French New Orleans,* 85.
70. Guenin-Lelle, *Story of French New Orleans,* 83, 88.
71. Thompson, *Exiles at Home,* 7.
72. Kmen, *Music in New Orleans,* 29.
73. *L'Advertiser,* March 19, 1835.
74. Johnson, *Congo Square in New Orleans,* 44.
75. Crutcher, *Tremé,* 26.
76. Dudley, *Building Antebellum New Orleans,* 15.
77. Logsdon and Bell, "Americanization of Black New Orleans," 207.
78. Couch, "Public Masked Balls," 421.
79. Dessens, *Creole City,* 136.
80. Dewulf, *From the Kingdom of Kongo to Congo Square,* 135–36.
81. Kinser, *Carnival, American Style,* 22.

82. *Daily Picayune,* March 18, 1841.

83. Atkins, *New Orleans Carnival Balls,* 16.

84. *New Orleans Daily Crescent,* April 22, 1850.

85. Dessens, *Creole City,* 212.

86. Ripley, *Social Life in Old New Orleans,* 116–20.

87. Olmsted, *A Journey in the Seaboard Slave States,* 586–87.

88. Olmsted, *The Cotton Kingdom,* 649.

89. Kinser, *Carnival, American Style,* 87–9.

90. *Daily Picayune,* March 19, 1853.

91. Johnson, *Congo Square in New Orleans,* 44.

92. Kmen, *Music in New Orleans,* 52.

93. *Daily Picayune,* March 19, 1858.

94. Parham, *American Routes,* 42.

95. Shaik, *Economy Hall,* 145.

96. Gotham, *Authentic New Orleans,* 37.

97. Dewulf, *From the Kingdom of Kongo to Congo Square,* 158.

98. John W. Blassingame, *Black New Orleans,* 15.

99. *Daily Picayune,* March 25, 1855.

100. Tregle, "Creoles and Americans," 161.

101. Couch, "Public Masked Balls," 407.

102. Dessens, *Creole City,* 107–8.

103. Tallant, *Mardi Gras,* 114.

104. Atkins, *New Orleans Carnival Balls,* 10–11.

105. An interesting side note is that the "Cowbellians" (or someone using their name) threw a masquerade ball on St. Joseph's Night at the Union Hall in 1853, three years before three of them ventured to New Orleans to form the Mistick Krewe of Comus, the first organized Carnival club. *Daily Picayune,* March 19, 1853.

106. Kmen, *Music in New Orleans,* 30.

107. Couch, "Public Masked Balls," 403.

108. *Daily Picayune,* March 20, 1857.

109. Dessens, *Creole City,* 85.

110. Dessens, *Creole City,* 211, 204, 199.

111. Potter, *A Hairdresser's Experience in High Life,* 22.

112. Gotham, *Authentic New Orleans,* 39.

113. Dudley, *Building Antebellum New Orleans,* 15.

114. *New Orleans Crescent,* March 3, 1859.

115. *Daily Crescent,* March 19, 1861.

116. *Daily Crescent,* February 18, 1861.

117. *Daily Picayune,* March 18, 1862.

4. OCCUPATION, RECONSTRUCTION, AND BEYOND

1. *Daily Picayune,* May 16, 1862.

2. Blassingame, *Black New Orleans,* 31–32.

3. Blassingame, *Black New Orleans,* 201.

4. Office of the Mayor, AA670, Permits issued by acting military mayor, 1864, City Archives & Special Collections, New Orleans Public Library.

5. Gushee, "Nineteenth-Century Origins of Jazz," 6.

6. Doyle, "Civilian Life in Occupied New Orleans."

7. Tallant, *Mardi Gras,* 123.

8. *Daily Picayune,* March 18, 1866; *Daily Picayune,* March 20, 1866.

9. *New Orleans Daily Crescent,* January 4, 1866.

10. Jacobs, "Benevolent Societies of New Orleans Blacks," 22.

11. Blassingame, *Black New Orleans,* 147.

12. *Daily Picayune,* March 17, 1867; March 19, 1867.

13. *Daily Picayune,* March 17, 1868; March 19, 1869.

14. *Daily Picayune,* March 19, 1870.

15. Taylor, *Louisiana Reconstructed,* 407–9.

16. Waud, "St. Louis Ball, N.O."

17. Benfey, *Degas in New Orleans,* 173.

18. Atkins, *New Orleans Carnival Balls,* 26, 158.

19. Johnson, *Slavery's Metropolis,* 207.

20. Atkins, *New Orleans Carnival Balls,* 158.

21. Benfey, *Degas in New Orleans,* 173.

22. Brook, *Accident of Color,* 142.

23. Mitchell, *All on a Mardi Gras Day,* 72.

24. Stewart, "Spirituality and Resistance," 191.

25. Kinser, *Carnival, American Style,* 70–71, 342.

26. Mitchell, *All on a Mardi Gras Day,* 74.

27. They were not part of the official Louisiana Militia according to the Jackson Barracks archives.

28. *New Orleans Times,* September 10, 1871.

29. Taylor, *Louisiana Reconstructed,* 62, 162, 163, 184, 283, 291.

30. Taylor, *Louisiana Reconstructed,* 415.

31. King, *The Great South, Vol. I,* 38, 43.

32. Taylor, *Louisiana Reconstructed,* 410.

33. *Daily Picayune,* March 20, 1874.

34. Mitchell, *All on a Mardi Gras Day,* 13.

35. Blassingame, *Black New Orleans,* 145.

36. Daggett, *Spiritualism in Nineteenth-Century New Orleans,* 134.

37. Shaik, *Economy Hall,* 135–36.

38. Shaik, *Economy Hall,* 325, 378.

39. *Daily Picayune,* March 20, 1874.

40. Benfey, *Degas in New Orleans,* 151, 180, 189.

41. Blassingame, *Black New Orleans,* 173.

42. Brook, *Accident of Color,* 52.

43. Atkins, *New Orleans Carnival Balls,* 73.

44. *Daily Picayune,* March 20, 1874.

45. Dixon Family Papers, Box 2, Amistad Research Center, Tulane University.

46. Prince, *The Ballad of Robert Charles,* 3.

47. Taylor, *Louisiana Reconstructed,* 70, 407–8.

48. *New Orleans Times,* March 20, 1879.

49. *Daily Picayune,* March 19, 1881.

50. *Daily Picayune,* March 20, 1874.

51. Kinser, *Carnival, American Style,* 139.

52. Sala, *America Revisited,* 102–3.

53. "Lent in New Orleans," WPA Papers, State Library of Louisiana, https://louisiana digitallibrary.org/islandora/object/state-lwp%3A4129.

54. Dunbar-Nelson, *The Goodness of St. Roch,* 36.

55. *Daily Picayune,* March 18, 1886.

56. LaCour, *New Orleans Masquerade,* 215.

57. Brook, *Accident of Color,* 257.

58. *Daily Picayune,* March 20, 1886.

59. *New Orleans States,* February 7, 1961.

60. *Daily Picayune,* February 22, 1881.

61. Rasmussen, ed., *A Girl's Life in New Orleans,* 94.

62. *Daily Picayune,* March 16, 1886.

63. *Daily Picayune,* March 20, 1888.

64. Atkins, "'Using the Bow and the Smile,'" 14.

65. Gotham, *Authentic New Orleans,* 93.

66. Atkins, "'Using the Bow and the Smile,'" 8.

67. Mitchell, *All on a Mardi Gras Day,* 25, 79.

68. Powell, *The Accidental City,* 221.

69. Da Matta, "An Interpretation of *Carnaval,*" 169.

70. Kinser, *Carnival, American Style,* 250.

71. Mitchell, *All on a Mardi Gras Day,* 100–101.

72. Mitchell, *All on a Mardi Gras Day,* 57.

73. Sala, *America Revisited,* 21–24.

74. *Daily Picayune* March 20, 1895.

75. *Times-Picayune,* March 18, 1895.

76. *Daily Picayune,* March 1, 1896.
77. Parham, *American Routes,* 46.
78. Prince, *Ballad of Robert Charles,* 6.
79. *Daily Picayune,* March 20, 1896.
80. *Daily Picayune,* March 20, 1898.
81. *Daily Picayune,* March 18, 1900.
82. *Times-Picayune,* March 19, 1901.
83. *Daily Picayune,* March 19, 1903; *Daily Picayune,* March 20, 1903.
84. *Daily Picayune,* March 20, 1904.
85. *Daily Picayune,* March 19, 1906; *Daily Picayune,* March 18, 1906.
86. *New Orleans Item,* November 30, 1906.
87. *Daily Picayune,* March 19, 1907; *New Orleans Item,* March 20, 1907.
88. *Daily Picayune,* March 20, 1909.
89. Poster from 1910, Historic New Orleans Collection.
90. *Daily Picayune,* March 20, 1911.
91. *Times-Democrat,* March 19, 1911.
92. *Daily Picayune,* March 20, 1912.
93. *New Orleans Item,* March 21, 1912.
94. *Times-Democrat,* March 16, 1913.
95. *New Orleans States,* March 18, 1919.
96. *New Orleans Item,* March 16, 1919.
97. Bedford-Jones, *Mardi Gras Mystery,* 89–90.
98. *Morning Tribune,* March 18, 1927.
99. Faber, *Building the Land of Dreams,* 19.
100. Kinser, *Carnival, American Style,* xx.

5. BLACK ST. JOSEPH'S NIGHT

1. Federal Writers' Project Papers, folder 25, Cammie G. Henry Research Center.
2. Hurston, *Mules and Men,* 183.
3. Dewulf, *From the Kingdom of Kongo to Congo Square,* 147.
4. Powell, *The Accidental City,* 97.
5. Herskovits, *Myth of the Negro Past,* 245–51.
6. Rightor, *Standard History of New Orleans,* 630.
7. Da Matta, "An Interpretation of *Carnaval,*" 169.
8. Gotham, *Authentic New Orleans,* 40–41.
9. Dewulf, *From the Kingdom of Kongo to Congo Square,* 123–24.
10. Power, *Impressions of America During the Years 1833, 1834, and 1835,* 250–54.
11. Deahl, "Buffalo Bill's Wild West Show in New Orleans," 289–98.
12. Berry, *Spirit of Black Hawk,* 103.

13. Latrobe, *Southern Travels,* 75.

14. Kirsch, *"Down Town" New Orleans in the Early "Eighties,"* 9–10.

15. Cable, *The Grandissimes,* 273.

16. Osborn, *All on a Mardi Gras Day* (documentary).

17. Osborn, *All on a Mardi Gras Day.*

18. Osborn, *All on a Mardi Gras Day.*

19. Stewart, "Spirituality and Resistance Among African Creoles," 194, 198.

20. Osborn, *All on a Mardi Gras Day.*

21. Kennedy, *Chief of Chiefs,* 63.

22. Sala, *America Revisited,* 92–3.

23. Kinser, *Carnival, America Style,* 232.

24. Dewulf, *From the Kingdom of Kongo to Congo Square,* 134.

25. Sala, *America Revisited,* 15, 93.

26. Stewart, "Spirituality and Resistance," 192.

27. Gotham, *Authentic New Orleans,* 94.

28. *New Orleans Item,* March 19, 1941.

29. Lyle Saxon, *Gumbo Ya-Ya,* 25.

30. Interview with Anthony Jeanjacques on May 19, 2020.

31. Medley, *Black Life in Old New Orleans,* 36–38.

32. Saxon, *Gumbo Ya Ya,* 11–14.

33. Federal Writers' Project Papers, folder 423, Cammie G. Henry Research Center.

34. Tallant, *Mardi Gras,* 240.

35. Kinser, *Carnival, American Style,* 135–36.

36. Federal Writers' Project Papers, folder 423, Cammie G. Henry Research Center.

37. A fan made of palm leaves.

38. Kirsch, *"Down Town" New Orleans in the Early "Eighties,"* 9–10.

39. Saxon, *Gumbo Ya-Ya,* 26.

40. Christian, "The Negro in Louisiana," 11.

41. McKinney, Federal Writers' Project Papers, folder 582, Cammie G. Henry Research Center.

42. Federal Writers' Project Papers, folder 423, Cammie G. Henry Research Center.

43. McKinney, "Captain Jackson Keeps the Baby Dolls from Strutting Their Stuff; Indians Come Out," 4, Federal Writers' Project Papers, folder 423, Cammie G. Henry Research Center.

44. McKinney, "Captain Jackson Keeps the Baby Dolls from Strutting Their Stuff; Indians Come Out," 4.

45. McKinney, "Captain Jackson Keeps the Baby Dolls from Strutting Their Stuff; Indians Come Out," 1–7.

46. *Times-Picayune,* March 17, 1940.

47. *Louisiana Weekly,* March 30, 1940.

48. *Louisiana Weekly,* March 16, 1940.

49. Kennedy, *Chief of Chiefs,* 78–79.

50. Clyde Kerr poster.

51. Kennedy, *Big Chief Harrison,* 150, 74–75, 123.

52. McKinney, Federal Writers' Project Papers, folder 423, Cammie Henry Research Center.

53. Kennedy, *Big Chief Harrison,* 297.

54. Kinser, *Carnival, American Style,* 197–99.

55. Gotham, *Authentic New Orleans,* 94.

56. Kennedy, *Chief of Chiefs,* 91–92.

57. Kennedy, *Chief of Chiefs,* 90–91.

58. Kennedy, *Big Chief,* 69, 7

59. Berry, *Spirit of Black Hawk,* 104.

60. Dewulf, *From the Kingdom of Kongo to Congo Square,* 168.

61. Kinser, *Carnival, American Style,* 137.

6. SICILIAN CELEBRATIONS

1. *New Orleans Item,* March 19, 1903.

2. *New Orleans Item,* June 13, 1902.

3. See "Mid-Lent vecchierelle (dessert)," La Valle del Metauro, https://www.lavalledelmetauro.it/contenuti/carnevale-feste-tradizioni-lavoro/scheda/7703.html.

4. Orso, "Sicilian Immigration into Louisiana," 603.

5. Soards City Directory of New Orleans, 1850.

6. A. V. Margavio and Jerome J. Salomone, *Bread and Respect,* 35–37.

7. Finley, Smith, and Duggan, *A History of Sicily,* 187–88.

8. Stewart, "Spirituality and Resistance," 184.

9. Margavio and Salomone, *Bread and Respect,* 65.

10. Margavio and Salomone, *Bread and Respect,* 182.

11. *New Orleans Republican,* March 8, 1872.

12. *New Orleans Republican,* March 11, 1875.

13. *Daily Picayune,* March 17, 1878.

14. *Daily Picayune,* March 19, 1881.

15. Jackson, *Dixie's Italians,* 63.

16. *Daily Picayune,* May 23, 1874.

17. Jackson, *Dixie's Italians,* 52.

18. Barnes and Breunlin, *Talk That Music Talk,* 116–17.

19. Coincidentally, Madame LaLaurie, the alleged perpetrator of the crimes at this address, was born on March 19.

20. Castellanos, *New Orleans as It Was,* 62, 163.

21. *Daily Picayune,* March 20, 1902.

22. Located in the Irish Channel neighborhood uptown.

23. *Daily Picayune,* March 20, 1906.

24. *New Orleans Item,* March 20, 1908.

25. *Daily Picayune,* March 18, 1908; *New Orleans Item,* March 20, 1908; *Daily Picayune,* March 20, 1908.

26. *Times-Picayune,* March 20, 1909.

27. *Daily Picayune,* March 20, 1912.

28. Juneau, *Celebrating with St. Joseph's Altars,* 2.

29. *New Orleans Item,* March 20, 1917.

30. Crowley, "Expansion of the St. Joseph's Altar in South Louisiana," vi., 85.

31. Tallant, "St. Joseph's Day," Federal Writers' Project Papers, folder 522, 4, Cammie G. Henry Research Center.

32. Orso, *St. Joseph Altar Traditions of South Louisiana,* 18.

33. State Library of Louisiana, WP000104, March 7, 1940.

34. Maude H. Wallace, April 1, 1940, Federal Writers' Project Papers, folder 120, Cammie G. Henry Research Center.

35. Margavio and Salomone, *Bread and Respect,* 164.

36. Crowley, "Expansion of the St. Joseph's Altar in South Louisiana," 9.

37. *Times-Picayune,* March 20, 1917.

38. *Times-Picayune,* March 20, 1919.

39. *Times-Picayune,* March 17, 1953.

40. *Times-Picayune,* March 19, 1919.

41. Kendall, *History of New Orleans,* 617.

42. *New Orleans Item,* March 17, 1923.

43. *New Orleans Item,* March 17, 1928.

44. Jacobs and Kaslow, *Spiritual Churches of New Orleans,* 118–19.

45. *New Orleans Item,* March 18, 1938.

46. *New Orleans States,* March 20, 1928.

47. "Louisiana, Orleans and St. Tammany Parish, Voter Registration Records, 1867–1905," FamilySearch (https://www.familysearch.org/ark:/61903/1:1:6Z58-JQ4N: Sat Mar 09 14:41:15 UTC 2024), Entry for Mrs. Lena Scovotto, November 14, 1928.

48. "Louisiana, Orleans and St. Tammany Parish, Voter Registration Records, 1867–1905." Entry for Rev. Lena Scovotto, December 5, 1941.

49. Daggett, *Spiritualism in Nineteenth-Century New Orleans,* 154–55.

50. McCullough, "A Day for St. Joseph: Food, Altars and New Orleans Style," *Washington Post,* March 14, 1995.

51. Maude H. Wallace, Federal Writers' Project, folder 120, Cammie G. Henry Research Center.

52. *New Orleans States,* April 2, 1940.

53. She said she usually paid the priest one dollar to bless her altar. Wallace, Federal Writers' Project Papers, folder 120, Cammie G. Henry Research Center.

54. Wallace, Federal Writers' Project Papers, folder 78, Cammie G. Henry Research Center.

55. *New Orleans Item,* March 18, 1952.

56. *New Orleans States-Item,* March 18, 1967.

57. *Times-Picayune,* March 17, 1968; *Dixie Magazine.*

58. *New Orleans States-Item,* March 19, 1970.

59. Jackson, *Dixie's Italians,* 154.

60. Crowley, "Expansion of the St. Joseph's Altar in South Louisiana," 30.

61. *Times-Picayune,* March 19, 1972.

62. Carnival parades used to wind through the French Quarter until the floats began to outgrow the ancient streets of the inner city.

63. *Times-Picayune,* March 18, 1979.

64. St. Francis Xavier St. Joseph Altar Society, *Viva San Giuseppe,* 2–4.

65. Orso, *The St. Joseph Altar Tradition,* 52.

CONCLUSION

1. Kein, *Gombo People,* 62.

2. Morton, "Creole Culture in the Poetry of Sybil Kein," 321–22.

Bibliography

ARCHIVAL COLLECTIONS

Amistad Research Center, Tulane University

Dixon Family Papers.

Cammie G. Henry Research Center, Northwestern State University of Louisiana

Federal Writers' Project Papers.

The Historic New Orleans Collection

Alfred R. Waud Collection.

William Russell Jazz Collection.

Jackson Barracks Military Library

Library of Congress

Louisiana Research Collection, Tulane University

John Minor Wisdom Collection, 1710–1960.

National Archives—Founders Online

New Orleans City Hall Archives

Cabildo Books.

New Orleans Public Library

City Archives & Special Collections.

Mayor's Permits 1864.

Lyle Saxon Papers.

Ordinances Conseil de Ville.

Soard's City Directory.

Robert Tallant Papers.

State Department of Archives and History

State Library of Louisiana

Louisiana Works Progress Administration (WPA) Papers.

University of New Orleans

Marcus Christian Collection.

University of Notre Dame Archives

Archdiocese of New Orleans, Colonial Correspondence.

NEWSPAPERS

Daily City Item
L'Abeille (*New Orleans Bee*)
L'Advertiser
Le Moniteur
Louisiana Weekly
Morning Tribune
New Orleans Crescent
New Orleans Daily Crescent
New Orleans Item
New Orleans Republican
New Orleans States
New Orleans States-Item
New Orleans Times
New Orleans Times-Picayune
New York Herald
Times-Democrat (New Orleans)
Washington Post

BOOKS AND ARTICLES

Adams, Thomas Jessen, and Matt Sakakeeny, eds. *Remaking New Orleans: Beyond Exceptionalism and Authenticity.* Duke University Press, 2019.

Armstrong, Louis. *Satchmo: My Life in New Orleans.* Da Capo Press, 1986.

Arthur, Stanley Clisby. *Old New Orleans.* Harmanson, 1954.

Asbury, Herbert. *The French Quarter: An Informal History of the New Orleans Underworld.* Basic Books, 2003.

Aslakson, Kenneth R. *Making Race in the Courtroom: The Legal Construction of Three Races in Early New Orleans.* New York University Press, 2014.

Atkins, Jennifer. "Using the Bow and the Smile': Old-Line Krewe Court Femininity in New Orleans Mardi Gras Balls, 1870–1920." *Louisiana History* 54, no. 1 (Winter 2013): 5–46.

———. *New Orleans Carnival Balls: The Secret Side of Mardi Gras, 1870–1920.* LSU Press, 2017.

Augustin, Donatien. *General Digest of the Ordinances and Resolutions of the Corporation of New Orleans.* J. Bayon, 1831.

Barnes, Bruce Sunpie, and Rachel Breunlin. *Talk That Music Talk: Passing on Brass Band Music in New Orleans the Traditional Way.* Center for the Book at the University of New Orleans, 2014.

Barthé, Darryl, Jr. *Becoming American in Creole New Orleans, 1896–1949.* LSU Press, 2021.

Baudier, Roger. *The Catholic Church in Louisiana.* Roger Baudier, 1939.

Bedford-Jones, H. *The Mardi Gras Mystery.* 1921; Resurrected Press, 2012.

Bell, Caryn Cossé. *Revolution, Romanticism, and the Afro-Creole Protest Tradition in Louisiana 1718–1868.* LSU Press, 1997.

———. "French Religious Culture in Afro-Creole New Orleans, 1718–1877." *U.S. Catholic Historian* 17, no. 2 (Spring 1999): 1–16.

Belmessous, Saliha. "Assimilation and Racialization in Seventeenth and Eighteenth-Century French Colonial Policy." *American Historical Review* 110, no. 2 (April 2005): 322–349.

Benfey, Christopher. *Degas in New Orleans: Encounters in the Creole World of Kate Chopin and George Washington Cable.* Alfred A. Knopf, 1997.

Berquin-Duvallon, M. *Travels in Louisiana and the Floridas in the Year 1802, Giving a Correct Picture of Those Countries.* Translated by John Davis. I. Riley and Company, 1806.

Berry, Jason. *The Spirit of Black Hawk: A Mystery of Africans and Indians.* University Press of Mississippi, 1995.

Biagetti, Samuel. "Enlightenment and Revolution: The Case of Louisiana, 1768." *Early American Studies* 12, no. 1 (2014): 68–92. http://www.jstor.org/stable/24474847.

Blackbird, Leila. "Entwined Threads of Red and Black: The Hidden History of Indigenous Enslavement in Louisiana, 1699–1824." Master's thesis, University of New Orleans, 2018.

Blassingame, John W. *Black New Orleans, 1860–1880.* University of Chicago Press, 1973.

Brasseaux, Carl A., and Glenn R. Conrad, eds. *The Road to Louisiana: The Saint-Domingue Refugees, 1792–1809.* Center for Louisiana Studies at the University of Southwestern Louisiana, 1992.

Brill, Mark. *Music of Latin America and the Caribbean.* Routledge, 2017.

Brook, Daniel. *The Accident of Color: A Story of Race in Reconstruction.* W. W. Norton, 2019.

Busi, Frederick. "Flaubert's Use of Saints' Names in *Madame Bovary.*" *Nineteenth Century French Studies* 19, no. 1 (Fall 1990): 95–109.

Cable, George W. *The Grandissimes: A Story of Creole Life.* Pelican Publishing, 2001.

Caillot, Marc-Antoine. *A Company Man: The Remarkable French-Atlantic Voyage of a Clerk for the Company of the Indies.* Edited by Erin M. Greenwald. Historic New Orleans Collection, 2013.

Callahan, Richard J., Jr., ed. *New Territories, New Perspective: The Religious Impact of the Louisiana Purchase.* University of Missouri Press, 2008.

Carpentier, Alejo. *The Kingdom of This World.* Translated by Pablo Medina. 1949; Farrar, Straus and Giroux, 2017.

Castellanos, Erick. "The Symbolic Construction of Community in Italy: Provincialism and Nationalism." *Ethnology* 49, no. 1 (2010): 61–78. http://www.jstor.org/stable/41410880.

Castellanos, Henry C. *New Orleans as It Was: Episodes of Louisiana Life.* L. Graham and Son, 1895.

Christian, Marcus. "The Negro in Louisiana." Collection of Marcus Christian, University of New Orleans.

Claiborne, W. C. C. *Official Letter Books of W.C.C. Claiborne, Volume 1, 1801–1816.* Edited by Dunbar Rowland. State Department of Archives and History, 1917.

Clark, Emily Suzanne. *A Luminous Brotherhood: Afro-Creole Spiritualism in Nineteenth Century New Orleans.* University of North Carolina Press, 2016.

Cole, Catherine. *The Story of the Old French Market, New Orleans.* New Orleans Coffee Company, n.d.

Conrad, Glenn R., ed. *Cross, Crozier and Crucible: A Volume Celebrating the Bicentennial of a Catholic Diocese in Louisiana.* Center for Louisiana Studies, 1993.

Costello, Brian J. *Carnival in Louisiana: Celebrating Mardi Gras from the French Quarter to the Red River.* LSU Press, 2017.

Couch, R. Randall. "The Public Masked Balls of Antebellum New Orleans: A Custom of Masque Outside the Mardi Gras Tradition." *Louisiana History* 35, no. 4 (Autumn 1994): 403–31.

Cowan, Walter Greaves, and Jack B. McGuire. *Louisiana Governors: Rulers, Rascals, and Reformers.* University Press of Mississippi, 2008.

Crété, Liliane. *Daily Life in Louisiana, 1815–1830.* Translated by Patrick Gregory. LSU Press, 1978.

Crowley, Nara Maria Ersilia. "The Expansion of the St. Joseph's Altar in South Louisiana." Master's thesis, Louisiana State University, 2010. https://digitalcommons.lsu.edu/cgi/viewcontent.cgi?article=3195&context=gradschool_theses.

Crutcher, Michael Eugene. *Tremé: Race and Place in a New Orleans Neighborhood.* University of Georgia Press, 2010.

Cuming, Fortescue. *Sketches of a Tour to the Western Country.* Cramer, Spear, and Eichbaum, 1810.

Daggett, Melissa. *Spiritualism in Nineteenth-Century New Orleans: The Life and Times of Henry Louis Rey.* University Press of Mississippi, 2017.

Da Matta, Roberto. "An Interpretation of *Carnaval.*" Translated by Ray Green. *SubStance* 11/12 (1982): 162–70. https://doi.org/10.2307/3684188.

Deahl, William E. "Buffalo Bill's Wild West Show in New Orleans." *Louisiana History* 16, no. 3 (1975): 289–98. http://www.jstor.org/stable/4231485.

Dee Das, Joanna. *Katherine Dunham: Dance and the African Diaspora.* Oxford University Press, 2017.

DeJean, Joan. *How Paris Became Paris: The Invention of the Modern City.* Bloomsbury, 2014.

———. *Mutinous Women: How French Convicts Became Founding Mothers of the Gulf Coast.* Basic Books, 2022.

Delany, Martin R. *Blake or, The Huts of America, A Corrected Edition.* Edited by Jerome McGann. Harvard University Press, 2017.

Dessens, Nathalie. *From Saint-Domingue to New Orleans: Migration and Influences.* University Press of Florida, 2007.

———. *Creole City: A Chronicle of Early American New Orleans.* University Press of Florida, 2015.

Dewulf, Jeroen. *From the Kingdom of Kongo to Congo Square: Kongo Dances and the Origins of the Mardi Gras Indians.* University of Louisiana at Lafayette Press, 2017.

Diner, Hasia R. *Hungering for America: Italian, Irish, and Jewish Foodways in the Age of Migration.* Harvard University Press, 2001.

Doyle, Elisabeth Joan, "Civilian Life in Occupied New Orleans, 1862–1865." (1955). *LSU Historical Dissertations and Theses,* 228. https://repository.lsu.edu/gradschool_disstheses/228.

Dubois, Laurent. *Haiti: The Aftershocks of History.* Metropolitan Books, 2012.

Dudley, Tara A. *Building Antebellum New Orleans: Free People of Color and Their Influence.* University of Texas Press, 2021.

Dunbar-Nelson, Alice Ruth Moore. *The Goodness of St. Roch.* Second Line Press, 2018.

Dunn, A. L. "Mardi Gras in New Orleans." 1930s. Louisiana Writers' Project, folder 82, Cammie Henry Research Center, Northwestern State University of Louisiana.

Durell, Edward Henry. *New Orleans as I Found It.* Harper's and Brothers, 1845.

Ebeyer, Pierre Paul. *Paramours of the Creoles.* Windmill Publishing, 1944.

Eccles, W. J. *France in America.* Harper & Row, 1972.

Endore, Guy. *Babouk.* Monthly Review Press, 1991.

Evans, Freddi Williams. *Congo Square: African Roots in New Orleans.* University of Louisiana at Lafayette Press, 2011.

Faber, Eberhard L. *Building the Land of Dreams: New Orleans and the Transformation of Early America.* Princeton University Press, 2015.

Falconer, Thomas, Henri De Tonti, and Robert Cavelier de la Salle. *On the Discovery of the Mississippi.* 1844; Shoal Creek Publishers, 1975.

Ferrer, Ada. *Freedom's Mirror: Cuba and Haiti in the Age of Revolution.* Cambridge University Press, 2014.

Fertel, Rien. "Charles Gayarré and the Imagining of an Exceptional City: The Literary Roots of the Creole City." In *Remaking New Orleans: Beyond Exceptionalism and Authenticity,* 55–74. Duke University Press, 2019.

Finley, M. I., Denis Mack Smith, and Christopher Duggan. *A History of Sicily.* Elisabeth Sifton Books, 1987.

Fischer, Roger A. *The Segregation Struggle in Louisiana, 1862–1877.* University of Illinois Press, 1974.

Flint, Timothy. *Recollections of the Last Ten Years.* Cummings, Hilliard, and Co., 1826.

Galignani, A., and W. Galignani. *New Paris Guide.* A. and W. Galignani and Co., 1846.

Garvey, Joan B., and Mary Lou Widmer. *Beautiful Crescent: A History of New Orleans.* New Garmer Press, 1982.

Genovese. Eugene D. *Roll, Jordan, Roll: The World the Slaves Made.* Vintage Books, 1976.

Giraud, Marcel. *A History of French Louisiana, Volume Five: The Company of the West Indies, 1723–1731.* Translated by Brian Pearce. LSU Press, 1991.

Gotham, Kevin Fox. *Authentic New Orleans: Tourism, Culture, and Race in the Big Easy.* New York University Press, 2007.

Gray, Ryan. "Rediscovering the 'Antiguo Cementerio': Archaeological Excavations and Recovery of Human Remains of the St. Peter Street Cemetery (16OR92)." Orleans Parish, Louisiana. Draft Report, August 2016.

Greer, Allan, ed. *The Jesuit Relations: Natives and Missionaries in Seventeenth-Century North America.* Bedford/St. Martin's, 2000.

Guenin-Lelle, Dianne. *The Story of French New Orleans: History of a Creole City.* University Press of Mississippi, 2016.

Gushee, Lawrence. "The Nineteenth-Century Origins of Jazz." *Black Music Research Journal* 14, no. 1 (1994): 1–24.

Hachard, Marie Madeleine. *The Letters of Marie Madeleine Hachard, 1727–28.* Translated by Myldred Masson Costa. Laborde Printing Co., 1974.

Hall, Gwendolyn Midlo. *Africans in Colonial Louisiana: The Development of Afro-Creole Culture in the Eighteenth Century.* LSU Press, 1992.

———. "The 1795 Slave Conspiracy in Pointe Coupée: Impact of the French Revolution." *Proceedings of the Meeting of the French Colonial Historical Society* 15 (1992): 130–41.

———. *Social Control in Slave Plantation Societies: A Comparison of St. Domingue and Cuba.* 1971; LSU Press, 1996.

Handbook of the Carnival, 1874. John W. Maulden, 1874.

Hanger, Kimberly S. "Personas de Varias Clases y Colores: Free People of Color in Spanish New Orleans, 1769–1803." PhD dissertation, University of Florida, 1991.

———. *Bounded Lives, Bounded Places: Free Black Society in Colonial New Orleans, 1769–1803.* Duke University Press, 1997.

Harvey, Paul. *Christianity and Race in the American South: A History.* University of Chicago Press, 2016.

Herskovits, Melville J. "African Gods and Catholic Saints in New World Negro Belief." *American Anthropologist* 39, no. 4 (1937): 635–43. http://www.jstor.org/stable/662418.

———. *The Myth of the Negro Past.* 1941; Beacon Press, 1990.

Hirsch, Arnold R., and Joseph Logsdon, eds. *Creole New Orleans: Race and Americanization.* LSU Press, 1992.

Homans, Jennifer. *Apollo's Angels: A History of Ballet.* Random House, 2010.

Hurston, Zora Neale. *Mules and Men.* First Perennial Library, 1990.

Iberville, Pierre Le Moyne d'. *Iberville's Gulf Journals.* Translated and edited by Richebourg Gaillard McWilliams. University of Alabama Press, 1981.

Jackson, Jessica Barbata. *Dixie's Italians: Sicilians, Race, and Citizenship in the Jim Crow Gulf South.* LSU Press, 2020.

Jacobs, Claude F. "Benevolent Societies of New Orleans Blacks During the Late Nineteenth and Early Twentieth Centuries." *Louisiana History* 29, no. 1 (1988): 21–33. http://www.jstor.org/stable/4232632.

Jacobs, Claude F., and Andrew J. Kaslow. *The Spiritual Churches of New Orleans: Origins, Beliefs, and Rituals of an African-American Religion.* University of Tennessee Press, 1991.

Johnson, James H. "Versailles, Meet Les Halles: Masks, Carnival, and the French Revolution." *Representations* 73, no. 1 (Winter 2001): 89–116.

———. "Urban Development and the Culture of Masked Balls in Nineteenth Century Paris." *Urban History* 40, no. 4 (November 2013): 646–62.

Johnson, Jerah. "Colonial New Orleans: A Fragment of the Eighteenth-Century French Ethos." In *Creole New Orleans: Race and Americanization,* 12–57. LSU Press, 1992.

———. *Congo Square in New Orleans.* Louisiana Landmarks Society, 1995.

Johnson, Paul Christopher. "Vodou Purchase: The Louisiana Purchase in the Caribbean World." In *New Territories, New Perspectives: The Religious Impact of the Louisiana Purchase,* 146–67. University of Missouri Press, 2008.

Johnson, Rashauna. *Slavery's Metropolis: Unfree Labor in New Orleans During the Age of Revolutions.* Cambridge University Press, 2016.

Jones, Linda Carol. *The Shattered Cross: French Catholic Missionaries on the Mississippi River, 1698–1725.* LSU Press, 2020.

Judge, Michael. *The Dance of Time: The Origins of the Calendar.* Arcade Publishing, 2004.

Juneau, Sandra Scalise. *Celebrating with St. Joseph's Altars: The History, Recipes, and Symbols of a New Orleans Tradition.* LSU Press, 2021.

Kein, Sybil. *Gombo People.* Leo J. Hall, 1981.

———, ed. *Creole: The History and Legacy of Louisiana's Free People of Color.* LSU Press, 2000.

Kendall, John Smith. *History of New Orleans, Volume I.* Lewis Publishing, 1922.

Kennedy, Al. *Big Chief Harrison and the Mardi Gras Indians.* Pelican Publishing, 2010.

———. *Chief of Chiefs: Robert Nathaniel Lee and the Mardi Gras Indians of New Orleans, 1915–2001.* Pelican Publishing, 2018.

King, Edward. *The Great South.* Arno Press, 1969.

Kinser, Samuel. *Carnival, American Style: Mardi Gras at New Orleans and Mobile.* University of Chicago Press, 1990.

Kirsch, Elise. *"Down Town" New Orleans in the Early "Eighties": Customs and Characters of the Old Robertson Street and Its Neighborhood.* Historic New Orleans Collections, 1951.

Kmen, Henry A. *Music in New Orleans: The Formative Years, 1791–1841.* LSU Press, 1966.

LaCour, Arthur Burton. *New Orleans Masquerade: Chronicles of Carnival.* Pelican Publishing, 1957.

Latrobe, Benjamin Henry. *The Journal of Latrobe: Being the Notes and Sketches of an Architect, Naturalist and Traveler in the United States from 1796 to 1820.* D. Appleton, 1905.

———. *Impressions Respecting New Orleans: Diary and Sketches, 1818–1820.* Edited by Samuel Wilson Jr. Columbia University Press, 1951.

Latrobe, John H. B. *Southern Travels: Journal of John H. B. Latrobe, 1834.* Edited by Samuel Wilson Jr. Historic New Orleans Collection, 1986.

Laussat, Pierre Clement de. *Memoirs of My Life.* Translated by Agnes Josephine Pastwa. LSU Press, 1978.

Le Clercq, Father Christian. *First Establishment of the Faith in New France, Volume 1.* Translated by John Gilmary Shea. John G. Shea, 1881.

Le Gardeur, René, Jr. *The First New Orleans Theatre, 1792–1803.* Leeward Books, 1963.

Lev, Elizabeth. *The Silent Knight: A History of St. Joseph as Depicted in Art.* Sophia Institute Press, 2021.

Lewis, Peirce F. *New Orleans: The Making of an Urban Landscape.* Ballinger Publishing, 1976.

Logsdon, Joseph, and Caryn Cossé Bell. "The Americanization of Black New Orleans, 1850–1900." In *Creole New Orleans: Race and Americanization,* 201–61. LSU Press, 1992.

Lomax, Alan. *Mr. Jelly Roll: The Fortunes of Jelly Roll Morton, New Orleans Creole and "Inventor of Jazz."* University of California Press, 2001.

Long, Charles H. "New Orleans as an American City: Origins, Exchanges, Materialities, and Religion." In *New Territories, New Perspective: The Religious Impact of The Louisiana Purchase,* 203–22. University of Missouri Press, 2008.

Margavio, A.V., and Jerome J. Salomone. *Bread and Respect: The Italians of Louisiana.* Pelican Publishing, 2002.

Martin, Joan M. "*Plaçage* and the Louisiana *Gens de Couleur Libre.*" In *Creole: The History and Legacy of Louisiana's Free People of Color,* 57–70. LSU Press, 2000.

Medley, Keith Weldon. *Black Life in Old New Orleans.* Pelican Publishing, 2014.

Mitchell, Reid. *All on a Mardi Gras Day: Episodes in the History of New Orleans Carnival.* Harvard University Press, 1995.

Morazan, Ronald R. "'Quadroon' Balls in the Spanish Period." *Louisiana History* 14, no. 3 (1973): 310–15. http://www.jstor.org/stable/4231338.

Morton, Mary L. "Creole Culture in the Poetry of Sybil Kein." In *Creole: The History and Legacy of Louisiana's Free People of Color,* 317–25. LSU Press, 2017.

Naipaul, V. S. *A Turn in the South.* Alfred A. Knopf, 1989.

Neidenbach, Elizabeth C. "Refugee from St. Domingue Living in This City: The Geography of Social Networks in Testaments of Refugee Free Women of Color in New Orleans." *Journal of Urban History* 42, no. 5 (2016): 841–62.

O'Gorman, John J. "Canada's Patron Saint." *Catholic Historical Review* 13, no. 4 (1928): 646–57.

Olmsted, Frederick Law. *A Journey in the Seaboard Slave States, with Remarks on Their Economy.* Dix and Edwards, 1856.

———. *The Cotton Kingdom: A Traveller's Observations on Cotton and Slavery in the American Slave States.* 1861; Alfred A. Knopf, 1966.

Orso, Ethelyn. *The St. Joseph Altar Traditions of South Louisiana.* Center for Louisiana Studies at the University of Southwestern Louisiana, 1990.

Orso, Ethelyn, and Peggy Kaveski. "Undisclosed Aspects of St. Joseph's Altars." *Louisiana Folklore Miscellany* 3, no. 5 (1975):14–18.

Osborn, Royce, director. *All on a Mardi Gras Day.* 2003; Spyboy Productions.

Osborne, Mitchel L. *Mardi Gras! A Celebration.* Picayune Press, 1981.

Ostendorf, Ann. "Louisiana Bohemians: Community and Creolization in the Colonial French Atlantic Roma Diaspora." https://www.academia.edu/42952043/Louisiana_Bohemians_Community_and_Creolization_in_the_Colonial_French_Atlantic_Roma_Diaspora?email_work_card=view-paper.

Parham, Angel Adams. *American Routes: Racial Palimpsests and the Transformation of Race.* Oxford University Press, 2017.

Pastor, Lori Renee. "Black Catholicism: Religion and Slavery in Antebellum Louisiana." Master's thesis, Louisiana State University, 2005. https://digitalcommons.lsu.edu/cgi/viewcontent.cgi?article=2863&context=gradschool_theses.

Pitot, James. *Observations on the Colony of Louisiana from 1796 to 1802.* LSU Press for the Historic New Orleans Collection, 1979.

Potter, Eliza. *A Hairdresser's Experience in High Life.* University of North Carolina Press, 2009.

Powell, Lawrence N. *The Accidental City: Improvising New Orleans.* Harvard University Press, 2012.

Power, Tyrone. *Impressions of America During the Years 1833, 1834, and 1835.* Samuel Bentley, 1836.

Prince, K. Stephen. *The Ballad of Robert Charles: Searching for the New Orleans Riot of 1900.* University of North Carolina Press, 2021.

Puckett, Newbell Niles. *The Magic and Folk Beliefs of the Southern Negro.* Dover Publications, 1969.

Radestock, Rudolph. *The Royal Ball-Room Guide.* W. Walker and Sons, 1877.

Rasmussen, Hans, ed. *A Girl's Life in New Orleans: The Diary of Ella Grunewald, 1884–1886.* LSU Press, 2023.

Reed, Adolph, Jr. "The Myth of Authenticity and Its Impact on Politics—in New Orleans and Beyond." In *Remaking New Orleans: Beyond Exceptionalism and Authenticity,* 307–25. Duke University Press, 2019.

Rightor, Henry, ed. *Standard History of New Orleans, Louisiana.* Lewis Publishing, 1900.

Ripley, Eliza. *Social Life in Old New Orleans: Being Recollections of My Girlhood.* D. Appleton, 1912.

Robertson, James Alexander. *Louisiana Under the Rule of Spain, France, and the United States, 1785–1807, Volume II.* Arthur H. Clark Co., 1911.

Robin, C. C. *Voyage to Louisiana, 1803–1805.* Translated by Stuart O. Landry Jr. Pelican Publishing, 1966.

Roediger, David R. *Working Towards Whiteness: How America's Immigrants Became White.* Basic Books, 2005.

Roussève, Charles Barthelemy. *The Negro in Louisiana: Aspects of His History and His Literature.* Xavier University Press, 1937.

Sala, George Augustus. *America Revisited: From the Bay of New York to the Gulf of Mexico, and from Lake Michigan to the Pacific.* Arno Press, 1974.

Sante, Luc. *The Other Paris.* Farrar, Straus and Giroux, 2015.

Saxon, Lyle. *Fabulous New Orleans.* D. Appleton-Century Co., 1943.

———. *Gumbo Ya-Ya: A Collection of Louisiana Folk Tales.* 1945; Pelican Publishing, 1998.

Schindler, Henri. *Mardi Gras: New Orleans.* Flammarion, 1997.

Scott, Julius S. *The Common Wind: Afro-American Currents in the Age of the Haitian Revolution.* Verso, 2018.

Shaik, Fatima. *Economy Hall: The Hidden History of a Free Black Brotherhood.* Historic New Orleans Collection, 2021.

Spear, Jennifer M. *Race, Sex, and Social Order in Early New Orleans.* Johns Hopkins University Press, 2009.

St. Francis Xavier St. Joseph Altar Society. *Viva San Giuseppe: Recipes of the St. Joseph Altar.* Society of St. Francis Xavier Church.

Stewart, John. "Spirituality and Resistance Among African-Creoles." In *New Territories, New Perspective: The Religious Impact of the Louisiana Purchase,* 168–202. University of Missouri Press, 2008.

Sublette, Ned. *The World That Made New Orleans: From Spanish Silver to Congo Square.* Lawrence Hill, 2009.

Tallant, Robert. *Mardi Gras.* Pelican Publishing, 1947.

———. *The Romantic New Orleanians.* E. P. Dutton, 1950.

Taylor, Joe Gray. *Louisiana Reconstructed, 1863–1877.* LSU Press, 1974.

Teja, Jesús F. de la. "St. James at the Fair: Religious Ceremony, Civic Boosterism, and Commercial Development on the Colonial Mexican Frontier." *The Americas* 57, no. 3 (2001): 395–416. http://www.jstor.org/stable/1007562.

Thompson, Shirley Elizabeth. *Exiles at Home: The Struggle to Become American in Creole New Orleans.* Harvard University Press, 2009.

Tilly, Charles. "Charivaris, Repertoires and Urban Politics." In *French Cities in the Nineteenth Century.* Routledge, 1981.

Tregle, Joseph G. "Creoles and Americans." In *Creole New Orleans: Race and Americanization,* 131–85. LSU Press,1992.

Twitty, Michael W. *The Cooking Gene: A Journey Through African American Culinary History in the Old South.* HarperCollins, 2017.

Usner, Daniel H., Jr. *Indians, Settlers, and Slaves in a Frontier Exchange Economy: The Lower Mississippi Valley Before 1783.* University of North Carolina Press, 1992.

Vidal, Cécile. *Caribbean New Orleans: Empire, Race, and the Making of a Slave Society.* University of North Carolina Press, 2019.

Virgets, Ronnie. *Saints and Lesser Souls: The New Orleans Views of Ronnie Virgets.* Feliciana Publishing, 2017.

Wall, Bennett H., and John C. Rodrigue, eds. *Louisiana: A History.* Wiley-Blackwell, 2014.

Walsh, William Shepard. *Curiosities of Popular Customs and of Rites, Ceremonies, Observances and Miscellaneous Antiquities.* J. B. Lippincott, 1897.

Wegmann, Andrew N. "The Vitriolic Blood of a Negro: The Development of Racial Identity and Creole Elitism in New Spain and Spanish New Orleans, 1763–1803." *Journal of Transatlantic Studies* 13, no. 2 (2015): 204–25. https://www.tandfonline.com/doi/full/10.1080/14794012.2015.1022373.

Whites, LeeAnn, and Alecia P. Long, eds. *Occupied Women: Gender, Military Occupation, and the American Civil War.* LSU Press, 2009.

Wilson, Samuel, Jr. *Bienville's New Orleans: A French Colonial Capital, 1718–1768.* Friends of the Cabildo.

The WPA Guide to New Orleans: The Federal Writers' Project Guide to 1930s New Orleans. Pantheon Books, 1938.

Young, Perry. *The Mistick Krewe: Chronicles of Comus and His Kin.* Carnival Press, 1931.

Index